Python in Depth

A Multipurpose Coder and Programmer's Guide

By

Nathan Venture, D

Thank You!

Table of Contents

Introduction: Embracing the Python Journey

Welcome to the fascinating world of Python programming, a realm that offers endless possibilities for creation, innovation, and problem-solving. Whether you're taking your first steps into programming, seeking to sharpen your coding skills, or looking to apply Python in professional settings, this journey promises to be as rewarding as it is enlightening. Python stands out for its simplicity, readability, and versatility, making it an excellent choice for beginners and a powerful tool for experienced developers.

The allure of Python isn't just in its ease of learning but also in its broad application across different fields. From web development to data analysis, machine learning, and beyond, Python has become the lingua franca for developers and data scientists alike. This book is designed to guide you through the variegated landscape of Python programming, from its basic constructs to more advanced concepts. Along the way, you'll find that Python's philosophy of simplicity and readability isn't just about making code easier to write but also about fostering a more inclusive and collaborative programming community.

Our journey into Python will start with laying down the foundation. Understanding the syntax, structure, and basic concepts of programming in Python is crucial. Emphasizing clarity, we'll explore variables, control structures, and functions, ensuring that you gain a solid grasp of these core principles. Python's syntax is designed to be readable and straightforward, emphasizing the importance of making code that's not only functional but also easy to understand by others.

Moving forward, we'll delve into more complex territories, exploring lists, dictionaries, and the power of comprehensions. These are the workhorses of Python programming, enabling you to manage data effectively and perform operations with minimal code. Here, you'll start to see Python's 'batteries included' philosophy in action, offering a rich standard library that allows you to focus on solving problems rather than reinventing the wheel.

Object-oriented programming (OOP) will be our next milestone. Python's support for OOP allows you to structure code in a way that is modular, reusable, and easy to understand. Through classes and objects, you'll learn to think about programming in terms of real-world entities and relationships, a fundamental shift that will open new vistas in how you approach coding tasks.

As we proceed, the journey will address the critical area of error handling and exception management, ensuring that your Python applications are robust and resilient. Learning to anticipate and manage errors gracefully is a hallmark of experienced developers, and Python's approach to exceptions will help you achieve this with clarity and elegance.

Writing idiomatic, or 'Pythonic', code is another critical aspect of your journey. Python's philosophy encourages coding styles that are not only efficient but also beautiful and expressive. You'll learn the subtleties of Pythonic code, including how adherence to the Zen of Python and the PEP 8 style guide can make your code more readable and enjoyable to work with.

Exploring Python's extensive selection of libraries and frameworks will be one of the most exciting parts of this journey. The ecosystem provides tools for web development, data analysis, machine learning, and more, making Python incredibly versatile. You'll get a taste of how to leverage these tools to build sophisticated applications and systems with less effort and more joy.

No modern programming education would be complete without touching upon the realms of file handling, I/O operations, and database interaction. Python simplifies these essential tasks, allowing you to manage files, communicate with databases, and even automate routine tasks with ease. These skills are foundational to many programming projects and will serve you well in your Python endeavors.

As we advance, you'll be introduced to the vibrant world of Python for data science, machine learning, and artificial intelligence. These are areas where Python truly shines, thanks to comprehensive libraries like NumPy, pandas, and TensorFlow. Here, your ability to manipulate data, train models, and glean insights from vast datasets will grow, aligning you with the cutting edge of technology and innovation.

Furthering your mastery, we'll explore the automation of tasks, web scraping, and the interaction of Python with the cloud, GUI programming, and even game development. Each of these chapters will build on your knowledge, showcasing Python's flexibility and power across different domains and platforms.

What sets Python apart isn't just its capabilities but also its community. Engaging with Python's vibrant community, contributing to open source projects, and continuously learning from the wealth of resources available are integral parts of the Python journey. This book will introduce you to these aspects, helping you become not just a Python programmer but an active participant in the Python ecosystem.

In conclusion, this journey through Python is designed to be comprehensive, insightful, and, above all, enjoyable. Regardless of your background, the goal is to imbue you with the skills, knowledge, and perspective needed to excel in your programming endeavors. By embracing the principles and practices presented herein, you'll find that Python offers not just a programming language but a pathway to innovation and discovery.

So let's embark on this journey together, exploring the depth and breadth of Python programming. Each chapter will bring new insights and challenges, pushing the boundaries of what you can achieve with Python. Through dedication and practice, you'll find that the Python journey is as enriching as it is essential to your growth as a programmer. Welcome to the world of Python, where every line of code brings you closer to becoming the developer you aspire to be.

Chapter 1:
The World of Python

Welcome to the expansive realm of Python, a versatile programming language that has significantly influenced the software development landscape. At the heart of Python's appeal is its straightforward syntax and readability, making it an ideal choice for beginners, while its powerful libraries and frameworks provide the tools needed for complex professional applications. This chapter delves into the reasons behind Python's popularity, shedding light on its myriad applications across different industries. From web development to artificial intelligence, Python's wide-ranging use cases illustrate its flexibility and capability to solve real-world problems. We'll also guide you through setting up your Python development environment, including selecting an Integrated Development Environment (IDE) that fits your project's needs. This setup is crucial for efficient coding and debugging, and with the right tools, you can streamline your workflow and focus on bringing your ideas to life. As we embark on this journey, remember that mastering Python opens doors to countless opportunities, whether you're aiming to advance your career, support academic pursuits, or explore personal projects.

Understanding Python's Popularity and Applications

Python's ascent in the world of technology is a testament to its versatility, readability, and robust community support. It's a language that has found a sweet spot in both introductory programming courses and advanced software engineering. The reasons behind Python's popularity are multifaceted, ranging from its simple syntax to the enormous library ecosystem that has grown around it. For beginners, Python's clear syntax resembles natural language, making it an accessible entry point into the complex world of programming.

The widespread adoption of Python across various industries can be largely attributed to its flexibility. Unlike languages that are specialized for certain tasks, Python is a general-purpose language. This means it can be used for web development, data analysis, artificial intelligence (AI), scientific computing, and more. Its versatility is further enhanced by the comprehensive selection of libraries and frameworks available, such as Django for web development, Pandas for data analysis, and TensorFlow for machine learning applications.

Another significant factor contributing to Python's popularity is its active and welcoming community. For those learning to code or developing complex systems, the community is a resource for learning, sharing, and collaboration. Numerous forums, social media groups, and local meetups provide avenues for engagement, support, and mentorship. This community support, combined with the extensive documentation available for Python and its libraries, eases the learning curve and problem-solving process.

From an educational standpoint, Python has become a favorite among academicians and students. Its simplicity allows educators to focus on teaching programming concepts rather than syntax nuances, making it an effective tool for teaching computational thinking. Additionally, Python's applications in scientific computing and data analysis align with academic research, where it is used for simulations, statistical analyses, and data visualization.

In the realm of web development, Python offers frameworks like Django and Flask, which have been used to build some of the world's most visited websites. These frameworks support rapid development and clean, pragmatic design, contributing to Python's reputation as an efficient tool for building scalable web applications.

Data analysis and machine learning represent areas where Python especially shines. Libraries such as NumPy and Pandas have established Python as the language of choice for data manipulation and analysis. For machine learning, libraries like TensorFlow, Keras, and Scikit-learn have made it easier for both beginners and professionals to implement complex algorithms and create sophisticated models.

Python's role in automation and scripting can't be understated. It's a powerful language for automating mundane or repetitive tasks, from simple file manipulations to large-scale network configuration. Python scripts can automate system administration tasks, data entry, and even email sorting, increasing efficiency and consistency.

The field of cybersecurity also benefits from Python's capabilities. Python is used for developing security tools, analyzing vulnerabilities, and automating tasks like traffic analysis and intrusion detection. The language's simplicity and efficiency make it an excellent choice for cybersecurity professionals who need to develop custom tools quickly.

In Internet of Things (IoT) projects, Python's readability and compact syntax make it a popular choice for developing applications that run on devices like the Raspberry Pi. Python's ability to interact with hardware, sensors, and networking systems facilitates the creation of smart devices and enables hobbyists and professionals alike to innovate in the IoT space.

The financial industry has embraced Python for quantitative and algorithmic trading, financial analysis, and cryptocurrency developments. Its libraries enable professionals to analyze market trends, develop trading strategies, and automate trading actions, showcasing Python's impact on fintech.

Python's influence extends to the creative domains of art, music, and digital content creation. It empowers artists, musicians, and creatives to express themselves through code, whether by generating visual art, composing music, or creating interactive experiences. The language's simplicity removes barriers to entry, allowing more people to explore creative coding and generative art.

Additionally, Python's role in education extends beyond computer science courses. It is increasingly used as a tool in scientific research, where its applications in data analysis, simulation, and visualization are invaluable. This makes Python a bridge between computational and traditional academic disciplines, fostering a multidisciplinary approach to education.

The future of Python looks bright, with ongoing development that promises more features, efficiency improvements, and an expanding ecosystem. As the language evolves, its community grows, continually enriching the resources and support available to programmers at all levels.

Understanding Python's popularity and its vast array of applications is crucial for beginners, intermediaries, and advanced users alike. It's not just about learning a programming language; it's about accessing a gateway to innumerable opportunities across different fields. Whether the aim is to develop web applications, analyze data, automate tasks, or create something entirely new, Python serves as a powerful ally in the world of technology.

In conclusion, Python's popularity is not a coincidence but a result of its versatility, ease of use, and the vibrant community that supports it. Its applications span across numerous industries, making it a valuable skill for any aspiring or practicing programmer. For those embarking on their Python journey, the path ahead is promising, filled with opportunities for innovation, learning, and making an impact.

Setting Up Your Python Environment

Embarking on your Python programming journey necessitates a foundational step: setting up your Python environment. This process involves selecting and installing Python on your computer, ensuring you have the most recent version to take advantage of the latest features and security enhancements. Equally important is choosing an Integrated Development Environment (IDE) or a code editor that matches your workflow preferences and project needs, a topic we delve into in the subsequent section. Additionally, familiarizing yourself with virtual environments will be pivotal in managing dependencies and avoiding conflicts between different Python projects. This initial setup phase is crucial as it lays the groundwork for a smooth and efficient development process, allowing you to focus on learning and building your projects with confidence. By equipping yourself with the right tools and understanding how to effectively organize your programming workspace, you're setting the stage for a rewarding Python coding experience.

Choosing an IDE (Integrated Development Environment)

Choosing and IDE is a crucial step for anyone looking to dive into the Python programming ecosystem effectively. An IDE can significantly enhance productivity by providing a cohesive environment packed with features that support the writing, testing, and debugging of code. The process of selecting an IDE, however, varies from one developer to another, depending on personal preference, project requirements, and levels of expertise.

Selecting an appropriate IDE is not merely about finding a tool that allows you to write code. It involves identifying an environment that meshes well with your workflow, offers compatibility with the libraries and frameworks you anticipate using, and scales with the complexity of your projects. For beginners, simplicity and ease of learning are often paramount, whereas seasoned developers might prioritize performance, customization, and advanced debugging capabilities.

When evaluating IDEs for Python development, it's essential to consider the community and support ecosystem surrounding the tool. A strong, active community can provide invaluable resources, from plugins and extensions to documentation and troubleshooting assistance. This aspect can dramatically increase your productivity and ease the learning curve associated with mastering a new development environment.

Among the most popular IDEs in the Python community are PyCharm, Visual Studio Code, and Jupyter Notebooks. PyCharm, developed by JetBrains, offers a rich feature set that caters to professional developers, including superior code analysis, a powerful debugger, and seamless integration with version control systems. Its comprehensive nature makes it an excellent choice for large-scale projects, although it might feel overwhelming to beginners.

Visual Studio Code, on the other hand, is a lightweight but powerful source code editor which runs on your desktop and is available for Windows, macOS, and Linux. It comes with built-in support for Python, and a vast library of extensions for other languages, debugging, and integrated terminal use. Its flexibility and performance make it a favorite among developers of all skill levels.

Jupyter Notebooks offer a unique approach by combining live code, equations, visualizations, and narrative text into interactive documents. This makes them particularly suited for data science, data analysis, and machine learning projects where a mix of code, output visualization, and documentation is beneficial.

Another aspect to consider is the platform support of the IDE, especially if you are working in a team or on projects that require cross-platform compatibility. Some IDEs are designed with a specific operating system in mind, while others are built to run across multiple platforms. Checking the compatibility of your chosen IDE with the operating systems you anticipate working on can save time and frustration.

For those who prefer a more stripped-down environment, or are working on smaller projects, simpler text editors like Sublime Text, Atom, or the classic Vim and Emacs, might be more suitable. These tools, while not offering the full array of features found in more comprehensive IDEs, can be customized with plugins and extensions to create a more tailored development experience.

Performance is another key factor to consider. IDEs can vary significantly in terms of the resources they require to run smoothly. Developers working on larger projects or those who use older hardware may need to pay particular attention to the efficiency of their chosen development environment to avoid unnecessary lags or crashes.

Integration capabilities with other tools and services are also critical. Consider whether the IDE supports direct integration with version control systems like Git, collaboration platforms such as GitHub, or continuous integration/continuous deployment (CI/CD) tools. These integrations can streamline your development process, making it more efficient and less prone to errors.

Customization and extensibility play a crucial role in fitting the IDE into your workflow rather than adjusting your process to fit the tool. The ability to install plugins, write custom scripts, or modify the interface can greatly enhance productivity and comfort. Investigate what customization options are available and how easily they can be implemented within your potential IDE choices.

Finally, the cost is an important consideration, especially for individual developers or small teams working with a limited budget. Some IDEs offer free community versions with fewer features, while others require a subscription or a one-time purchase. Evaluating the cost against the features offered can help you make a financially sound decision.

In conclusion, choosing the right IDE for your Python development is a multifaceted decision that should be made based on personal workflow preferences, the nature of the projects you intend to work on, and the level of support you expect from the community. Experimenting with a few different IDEs, starting with the ones mentioned above, can provide a practical way to find the environment that best suits your needs. Remember, the ideal IDE is one that not only makes coding more efficient and enjoyable but also supports your growth as a developer by offering the tools and resources you need to tackle increasingly challenging problems.

Remember, the process of selecting an IDE is highly personal and subject to change as you evolve as a programmer. There's no "one size fits all" solution, and what works best for you now might change as your projects, experience, and preferences develop. Stay open to exploring new tools and approaches, and be ready to adapt your environment to best support your journey in Python programming.

Chapter 2: Python Basics: Syntax and Structure

Embarking on the journey from the general landscape of Python into the specifics of its syntax and structure, chapter two lays the foundation necessary for all programmers, whether they are just starting with Python or looking to solidify their understanding of its core mechanisms. Python's philosophy encapsulates readability and simplicity, which is evident in its syntax that aims to be clean and expressive. This chapter delves deep into the fundamental building blocks of Python programming, covering how variables and data types work in Python to store and manage information efficiently. Readers will gain insights into Python's dynamic typing system and how it contrasts with statically typed languages, making Python particularly flexible and powerful for a wide range of applications. With a focus on control structures such as the conditional statements **if**, looping mechanisms **for**, and **while**, the section primes readers on directing the flow of their programs, allowing them to solve more complex problems. Additionally, it introduces the concept and utility of functions in Python, emphasizing the importance of code reusability and modular programming. By the end of this chapter, readers will be well-equipped with an understanding of Python's syntax and structure, setting a sturdy platform for exploring more advanced topics in subsequent chapters.

Variables and Data Types

Moving on from the foundations of Python's syntax and its vast applications, it's essential to dive into the core elements that you'll interact with on a daily basis: variables and data types. Understanding these components is pivotal for anyone aiming to master Python, be it for software development, data science, or personal projects. Variables in Python can be thought of as names attached to particular values or objects, allowing for more dynamic and readable code.

At its simplest, a variable can hold a value, such as a number or a string. For instance, when you assign **a = 5**, you're declaring a variable named **a** and assigning it the value of **5**. This action is straightforward but powerful, providing the foundational mechanism for manipulating data within your programs. Python is dynamically typed, meaning you don't need to explicitly declare a variable's type before using it. The interpreter infers the type automatically based on the assigned value, enhancing flexibility and increasing coding efficiency.

Data types in Python are categorical ways to classify the kind of data a variable holds. The primary types are integers, floating-point numbers, strings, and booleans. Each of these types serves different purposes. For example, integers are whole numbers, floating-point numbers contain decimal points, strings represent textual data, and booleans indicate **True** or **False** values.

Understanding integers and floating-point numbers is crucial for performing arithmetic operations, which are common in almost every Python script. These data types handle numerical calculations, with floats being used when more precision is required. It's also important to note how Python handles division; dividing two integers automatically results in a float to preserve the precision of the result.

Strings in Python are quite versatile and can be defined either by using single (' '), double (" "), or triple (''' ''' or """ """) quotes. The choice between single or double quotes typically comes down to personal preference or the need to include quotes within the string itself. Triple quotes are particularly useful for multi-line strings, allowing for the creation of complex textual data effortlessly.

Booleans, while seemingly simple, play a critical role in control structures and decision-making within programs. They are the outcome of comparison or logical operations, guiding the flow of execution based on conditions being **True** or **False**.

Additionally, Python supports more complex data types such as lists, dictionaries, tuples, and sets. These data structures are essential for organizing data in a way that is both efficient and intuitive. Lists, for instance, are ordered collections that can store a variety of object types, including other lists. Dictionaries store key-value pairs, providing a fast way to retrieve data using keys.

Understanding the type of data and how to manipulate these types is fundamental. Python provides various functions and methods to convert between data types, such as **int()** to convert to an integer, **float()** to convert to a floating-point number, and **str()** to convert to a string. Such conversions are often necessary for data processing and manipulation tasks.

It's also worth noting Python's dynamic nature allows variables to change types through reassignment. This feature can be beneficial, but it requires careful management to avoid unexpected behavior or errors in your code. Explicitly converting between types, as needed, can help maintain clarity and predictability.

The immutability of certain data types, like strings and tuples, is another vital concept. Once an immutable object is created, it can't be altered. Attempting to change such an object will result in the creation of a wholly new object. Understanding immutability is crucial when working with these types, especially in contexts where performance and memory management are concerns.

Variable naming conventions in Python follow a few simple rules and recommendations. Names should be descriptive, making your code more readable and maintainable. Python uses snake_case as the preferred way to name variables, which involves lowercasing letters and separating words with underscores. Following these guidelines helps ensure that your code adheres to Python's philosophy of readability and simplicity.

In summary, mastering variables and data types is a cornerstone of proficient Python programming. This knowledge enables you to manipulate data effectively, write clearer and more efficient code, and understand the operations and transformations applied to your data. As you progress, these concepts will form the foundation for understanding more complex data structures and algorithms.

As we move forward, remember that practice is key to internalizing these concepts. Experimentation with different data types, conversion methods, and variable assignments will reinforce your understanding and skillset. Python's interactive nature makes it an excellent language for such exploration, encouraging you to test and learn in a dynamic environment.

In conclusion, variables and data types are the basic building blocks of Python programming. They allow you to store, manipulate, and retrieve information in a variety of ways, paving the way for more complex and powerful applications. With a solid understanding of these concepts, you're well on your way to becoming proficient in Python and ready to tackle more advanced topics.

Control Structures: If, For, While

Control structures are the backbone of programming in Python, allowing for the dynamic execution of code blocks based on certain conditions or the repeated execution of a code block. This section will dive into 'if', 'for', and 'while' statements, providing the groundwork for making decisions within your programs and controlling the flow of execution.

The 'if' statement is your primary tool for branching in Python. It allows your program to execute a certain block of code only if a specified condition is true. It's akin to a crossroad where the program must choose which path to follow based on the condition provided. For instance, an 'if' statement can be used to check if a user's input is a certain value before taking action accordingly.

Following the 'if' statement, we have the 'elif' and 'else' statements to provide additional conditions and a default action when none of the conditions are met. This trio allows for comprehensive decision-making in your code. Utilizing these effectively can lead to more readable, efficient programs that behave exactly as intended under a variety of scenarios.

Looping in Python is primarily done using 'for' and 'while' constructs. The 'for' loop is particularly powerful in Python, used for iterating over the elements of a sequence whether it be a list, tuple, dictionary, set, or string. This makes 'for' loops incredibly versatile, enabling one to execute a block of code for each element in the sequence.

An example use of a 'for' loop could be iterating over a list of numbers and printing each number doubled. Python's 'for' loop is distinct in its readability and ease of use, especially with complex data structures.

The 'while' loop, on the other hand, repeats as long as a certain boolean condition remains true. It's ideal for scenarios where you need to loop until a specific condition changes, such as waiting for user input or monitoring data until it reaches a particular state.

Both 'for' and 'while' loops can be controlled further through the use of 'break' and 'continue' statements. 'break' allows for an immediate exit from the loop, while 'continue' skips to the next iteration of the loop. This provides enhanced control over loop execution and can help avoid infinite loop situations that could crash a program.

In addition to basic control structures, Python offers list comprehensions, which provide a concise way to create lists based on existing lists. While not a control structure per se, list comprehensions are built upon the fundamentals of 'for' loops and offer a powerful, readable alternative to traditional loop statements.

Python's control structures are not just limited to simple data types. They also extend to more complex structures, allowing for deep levels of nesting and manipulation. For instance, nested 'if' statements or loops can address multi-dimensional arrays or more complex decision trees.

Understandably, the use of control structures comes with the responsibility of writing clean, maintainable code. Deep nesting can lead to code that's difficult to read and maintain. Python encourages the use of simple, effective lines of code, and adhering to this principle can lead to better, more efficient programming.

Error handling is an essential aspect of working with control structures. Python provides try-except blocks as a way to catch and handle errors gracefully. While not a control structure in the traditional sense, understanding how your 'if', 'for', and 'while' loops interact with potential errors is crucial for writing robust Python programs.

The power of Python's control structures becomes evident when applied to real-world problems. Whether it's filtering data, performing calculations, or automating repetitive tasks, understanding how to effectively use 'if', 'for', and 'while' statements is pivotal.

Exercises and practical examples are instrumental in mastering these concepts. Implementing control structures in small programs will cement your understanding and prepare you for more complex scenarios. Python's philosophy of readability and simplicity makes it an excellent language for learning these fundamental programming concepts.

In summary, control structures in Python form the foundation upon which complex, efficient, and effective programs are built. By understanding and applying 'if', 'for', and 'while' statements, you'll be well-equipped to tackle a wide range of programming challenges. Remember, the elegance of Python lies in its simplicity and readability, qualities that extend deeply into its control structures.

As we move forward into understanding functions in the next section, remember that control structures often form the logic within functions, further emphasizing their importance in Python programming. Combining control structures with functions, as we'll see, enables even more powerful and modular code, leading to well-organized, maintainable, and efficient programs.

Functions: Defining and Using

In our journey through Python Basics, after exploring variables, data types, and control structures, we arrive at one of the most powerful aspects of programming in Python – functions. Functions are at the heart of Python programming, allowing programmers to encapsulate code within reusable blocks. This abstraction not only makes our code more readable and maintainable but also allows us to solve complex problems more efficiently.

At its core, a Python function is defined using the *def* keyword, followed by a function name, parentheses, and a colon. Inside these parentheses, we can pass zero or more parameters. The body of the function is indented underneath the definition. Functions can perform actions and also return a result using the *return* keyword. If no return statement is present, the function will return **None**.

Let's illustrate this with an example:

```
def greet(name):
return "Hello, " + name + "!"
```

In this simple example, *greet* is a function that takes a single parameter *name* and returns a greeting as a string. The power of this function becomes evident when we realize we can now greet anyone without writing the greeting template again.

Utilizing functions properly involves understanding several key concepts including parameters, arguments, and the return values. Parameters are the variables listed inside the parentheses in the function definition, while arguments are the values that are sent to the function when it is called. This distinction is subtle but important for writing clear code.

Python functions can also have default parameter values, making some arguments optional during a function call. This feature adds flexibility to our functions, allowing them to handle different use cases more gracefully. Here's how you might define a function with a default value:

```
def greet(name="World"):
return "Hello, " + name + "!"
```

In this variant of the *greet* function, if no argument is provided, "World" is used as the default greeting name. Default parameters enable functions to be called with fewer arguments.

Beyond simple return types, Python functions can return multiple values. This might surprise programmers coming from other languages where functions are strictly limited to one return value. In Python, multiple values are returned as tuples:

```
def get_min_max(numbers):
return min(numbers), max(numbers)
```

This function, *get_min_max*, takes a list of numbers as an argument and returns both the minimum and maximum values found within that list. Utilizing tuple unpacking, we can easily capture these multiple return values separately:

```
min_val, max_val = get_min_max([1, 2, 3, 4,
5])
```

Another advanced feature of Python functions is the use of ***args** and ****kwargs** to pass a variable number of arguments to a function. This is particularly useful when you aren't sure how many arguments might be passed to your function or if you want to accept keyword arguments.

When defining functions, it's also imperative to document their behavior clearly. Python supports documentation via docstrings – multi-line strings within the function that describe its purpose, parameters, return values, and any exceptions it might raise. Well-documented code is not only a boon for others but for your future self as well.

In practical programming, custom functions are invaluable. They allow you to segment your code into manageable pieces, each doing its specific task. This segmentation leads to code that is easier to debug, test, and extend. Moreover, functions facilitate code reuse, a key aspect of efficient coding practices.

As we continue expanding our Python knowledge, we'll see that functions play a crucial role in more advanced topics such as decorators, closures, and functional programming concepts.

Understanding and mastering the use of functions is a significant step towards leveraging the full power of Python.

In summary, functions in Python are defined to perform a specific task, can return values, and can take parameters. They improve the clarity and reusability of your code, reduce duplication, and make it more organized. As you develop more intricate programs, you'll appreciate the simplicity and effectiveness that functions bring to your coding toolkit.

With a firm grasp on defining and using functions, you're now better prepared to explore the complexities of Python programming. Remember, practice is key. Try creating your own functions, experimenting with different parameter types, and see how they can make your code cleaner and more efficient.

Chapter 3: Python Intermediate: Lists and Dictionaries

As we delve into the world of Python beyond the basics, we encounter two powerful data structures integral to effective coding and problem-solving: lists and dictionaries. These structures allow for more organized, efficient, and sophisticated manipulation of data, paving the way for more complex and dynamic Python applications. A list in Python is an ordered collection of items that can be altered or changed, offering flexibility in storing sequences of values. Their versatility shines through in tasks ranging from simple item enumeration to more complex operations like sorting and reversing elements. Dictionaries, on the other hand, store data in key-value pairs, providing a way to associate unique keys with values. This makes data retrieval straightforward and fast, especially when dealing with large datasets where quick access to information is crucial.

Understanding how to effectively utilize lists and dictionaries is foundational for Python programmers aiming to enhance their coding toolkit. Whether it's iterating over data, performing searches, or manipulating information, mastering these structures will greatly augment a developer's capacity to write clean, efficient, and Pythonic code. This chapter aims to equip readers with the knowledge to not only work with lists and dictionaries but also to understand the under-the-hood mechanisms that make them so efficient and versatile. Through examples and explanations, we will explore the nuances of these data types, including when and why to use them, thereby solidifying their role in Python programming for tasks ranging from data analysis to software development.

Working with Lists

As we delve into the world of Python's data structures, lists stand out for their versatility and efficiency in handling ordered collections of items. They serve as a fundamental aspect of Python programming, offering a plethora of functionalities that cater to various computational tasks. This chapter is tailored to enhance your proficiency in working with lists, enabling you to manipulate and leverage them in a myriad of contexts.

At its core, a list in Python is a sequence of elements, each identified by an index. The flexibility to store different data types, including integers, strings, and even other lists, makes it a powerful tool for developers. Understanding the basic operations such as creating lists, accessing elements, and slicing sublists is the first step toward mastering this versatile data structure.

To create a list, one simply encloses items in square brackets, separated by commas. This straightforward syntax eases the process of list initialization and manipulation. For instance, initializing a list of prime numbers or a list of student names is accomplished with minimal code. Furthermore, Python's dynamic typing allows lists to contain elements of different types, enhancing their flexibility.

Accessing elements in a list is an operation frequently encountered in Python programming. By utilizing indexes, one can retrieve or modify items within a list. It's important to note that Python indexes start at 0, meaning the first element is accessed with index 0. This indexing system is crucial for efficient list manipulation, including iterating over elements and extracting specific items.

Alongside basic operations, slicing is a feature that adds to the robustness of list handling in Python. Slicing enables the extraction of sublists from a broader list, using a colon notation to specify start and end positions. This functionality is invaluable for tasks that require manipulation of data segments, such as in data analysis or when working with sequences.

The addition and removal of elements are operations that highlight the dynamic nature of lists in Python. Methods such as *append()*, *insert()*, *pop()*, and *remove()* allow for efficient modification of lists, facilitating operations like concatenation, element insertion at a specific index, and deletion of elements based on value or index.

Sorting and reversing lists are common tasks that benefit from Python's built-in methods. The *sort()* method rearranges the elements of a list in ascending or descending order, based on specified criteria. This is especially useful in data organization and preparation for analysis. Similarly, the *reverse()* method changes the order of elements in a list, enabling operations that require such transformations.

For scenarios where list iteration is necessary, Python offers a clear and concise syntax. The *for* loop, in conjunction with the *in* keyword, allows for elegant traversal of list items, making code readable and maintainable. This is particularly beneficial in tasks that involve element-wise operations or when filtering items based on certain conditions.

Python also supports list comprehensions, a concise way to create lists. These expressions allow for the transformation of one list into another, applying an expression to each item while optionally filtering on a condition. List comprehensions are a testament to Python's ability to provide powerful functionalities in a succinct and expressive syntax.

The concept of list comprehensions extends beyond just simplification of code. It embodies Python's philosophy of emphasizing readability and efficiency. Through examples and exercises, one can appreciate the elegance and power of list comprehensions for tasks such as generating sequences or transforming data structures.

Another advanced feature of lists in Python is the ability to nest lists within each other. This facilitates the representation of more complex data structures like matrices or graphs. Understanding how to access and manipulate nested lists is crucial for applications in scientific computing, game development, and data analysis.

Working with lists also involves understanding their performance implications. Operations such as appending elements at the end of a list are generally fast, while inserting elements at the beginning or middle can be slower due to the need to shift other elements. Knowledge of these characteristics is essential for writing efficient Python code, especially in performance-critical applications.

Finally, the list's role in Python's ecosystem is reinforced by its integration with other data structures and functionalities. Whether it's converting between lists and other types like strings or sets, or utilizing lists in conjunction with file operations, understanding lists is foundational to Python programming.

As we conclude this exploration of working with lists, it's clear that mastering this data structure opens up a myriad of possibilities for solving real-world problems. Through practical examples, exercises, and a systematic approach to learning, one can leverage lists to their full potential, contributing significantly to their repertoire of Python programming skills.

In summary, the journey through working with lists is a microcosm of programming in Python—showcasing versatility, efficiency, and elegance. With a solid grasp of lists, you are well-equipped to tackle more complex data structures and algorithms, paving the way for advanced studies and professional applications of Python.

Exploring Dictionaries

In this section, we delve into dictionaries, an essential data structure in Python that enables efficient data storage and retrieval by key. Dictionaries, often termed associative arrays in other programming languages, store data as key-value pairs where each unique key points to a value. This structure is particularly useful for tasks that require quick access to elements without the need for ordered sequences.

Dictionaries are defined with curly braces ***{}***, with key-value pairs separated by commas, and keys and values linked by colons. For instance, ***{'name': 'John', 'age': 30}*** illustrates a simple dictionary containing a person's name and age. Keys are typically strings, but immutable types such as numbers and tuples can also serve as keys, offering flexibility in how data is organized.

Creating a dictionary is straightforward, yet its power lies in its ability to quickly add, delete, and modify key-value pairs. This mutable nature makes dictionaries apt for situations where data is dynamic, and changes are frequent. To add a new key-value pair, simply assign a value to a new key, like ***dict['new_key'] = 'value'***.

Retrieving values is equally simple: ***dict['name']*** would return 'John'. If a key does not exist, however, Python raises a KeyError, emphasizing the need for either checking key existence or using the ***get()*** method. ***get()*** returns the value for a key if it exists, or a default value (None, if not specified) otherwise, thus avoiding exceptions.

Removing key-value pairs can be done using the ***del*** statement or the ***pop()*** method. While ***del dict['name']*** removes the key 'name' and its associated value from the dictionary, ***dict.pop('name')*** also returns the value, offering additional control over the removal process.

Iterating over dictionaries showcases their versatility. One can iterate over keys, values, or key-value pairs. The methods ***keys()***, ***values()***, and ***items()*** are instrumental in these operations, making it possible to loop through dictionaries in various ways to access and manipulate data efficiently.

Dictionaries also support comprehensions, a powerful feature for succinctly creating dictionaries from sequences or transforming existing dictionaries. For example, ***{k: v for k, v in some_list}*** dynamically creates a dictionary from a list of tuples.

Another notable feature is the handling of missing keys with the ***setdefault()*** and ***defaultdict*** from the collections module. These tools provide defaults for keys that are not in the dictionary, simplifying the management of dictionary entries and avoiding key errors.

Nesting dictionaries offers a way to structurally organize complex data. By storing dictionaries within dictionaries, one can model hierarchical or multidimensional data, a technique often employed in data manipulation and analysis tasks.

Dictionaries are not just isolated data structures but can be linked with lists, sets, and even other dictionaries, to form complex data models that can be navigated and manipulated with Python's expressive syntax. This integration makes programming in Python both an efficient and enjoyable endeavor.

The performance of dictionaries is another key aspect. Due to their implementation based on hash tables, dictionaries offer O(1) time complexity for lookup, insertion, and deletion operations under average cases. This efficiency is pivotal in applications that demand rapid access to large datasets.

Working with dictionaries reveals Python's commitment to clean, readable, and expressive code. The language's syntax and design philosophies, such as the Zen of Python, emphasize simplicity and the importance of making coding intuitive and accessible.

In practical applications, dictionaries find extensive use in data analysis, web development (especially in frameworks like Django and Flask where they're used to pass data to templates), and configuration management among others. Their adaptability to various data representations and manipulations makes them indispensable in the Python programmer's toolkit.

Security considerations become relevant when using dictionaries, especially concerning user-generated keys. It's crucial to validate or sanitize inputs that may become dictionary keys to avoid injection attacks or unintended behavior. Python's dynamic nature offers flexibility but demands vigilance in handling potentially unsafe operations.

In summary, dictionaries are a cornerstone of Python programming, offering a robust and flexible structure for data storage and manipulation. By mastering dictionaries, programmers can effectively tackle a wide range of programming challenges, streamline their code, and implement sophisticated data handling mechanisms. The subsequent sections will build upon these foundational concepts, exploring more advanced data structures and Python features.

Comprehensions for Simplifying Code

One of the most powerful, yet underutilized, features in Python's repertoire for handling lists and dictionaries is comprehension. Comprehensions provide a concise, readable way to create lists, dictionaries, and sets. This section delves into how comprehensions can simplify your code, make it more Pythonic, and potentially improve its performance.

At their core, comprehensions are syntactic sugar for the traditional loops used in generating collections in Python. A list comprehension, for example, allows you to generate a new list by applying an expression to each item in an iterable. The beauty of comprehensions lies in their ability to condense several lines of code into a single, readable line.

To understand the subtlety and power of comprehensions, let's consider a task as simple as squaring numbers. Without comprehensions, you might use a for loop to iterate over a list and append the square of each number to a new list. However, with list comprehension, this operation becomes a one-liner: **[x**2 for x in range(10)]**, generating the squares of numbers 0 through 9.

Similarly, dictionary comprehensions offer a streamlined way to construct dictionaries. By iterating over key-value pairs, you can dynamically build dictionaries without the boilerplate code required by loops. For instance, creating a dictionary that maps numbers to their squares can be succinctly achieved with **{x: x**2 for x in range(10)}**.

Comprehensions also support conditionals, which further enhances their utility. You can filter items from the input list or sequence on which the comprehension is based, providing a powerful tool for creating complex collections in a straightforward way. For example, **[x for x in range(10) if x % 2 == 0]** generates a list of even numbers between 0 and 9.

While comprehensions are powerful, it's essential to use them judiciously. Extremely complex or nested comprehensions can be hard to read, defeating the purpose of simplifying code. As a rule of thumb, if your comprehension spans more than two lines or is difficult to understand at a glance, it may be wise to consider using traditional loops for clarity.

The performance of comprehensions is another aspect worth noting. Generally, comprehensions are faster than equivalent code written using loops. This speed advantage is due to the optimized C implementation in Python's interpreter. However, the performance gain might not be noticeable for small datasets or simple operations.

It's also important to understand that comprehensions are not a one-size-fits-all solution. While they excel at creating new collections from existing ones, comprehensions should not be used to perform side effects, such as manipulating global state or modifying the input collection. For these tasks, explicit for loops are more appropriate.

Another aspect to consider is the scope of variables inside comprehensions. Variables defined in a comprehension are local to the expression. This scoping rule helps prevent unexpected side effects and conflicts with variables outside the comprehension.

To master comprehensions, it's helpful to practice by refactoring existing code. Take a piece of code that uses loops to generate lists or dictionaries and attempt to rewrite it using comprehensions. This exercise not only reinforces the syntax but also improves your ability to think in a more Pythonic way.

Interestingly, the concept of comprehensions is not unique to Python. Many functional programming languages offer similar constructs, reflecting the influence of functional programming paradigms on Python's design. Understanding comprehensions can thus also ease the transition to or from other languages with similar features.

In conclusion, comprehensions are a valuable tool for any Python programmer, from beginners to seasoned veterans. By leveraging comprehensions to their full potential, you can write cleaner, faster, and more Pythonic code. Like any powerful tool, the key is to use comprehensions wisely—balancing readability, maintainability, and performance to create elegant solutions to complex problems.

As we move forward, keep in mind that Python offers many such features designed to simplify coding tasks. By embracing these features and incorporating them into your coding practices, you'll continue to grow as a Python programmer, capable of tackling an increasingly broad array of challenges with confidence and skill.

Chapter 4:
Python Advanced: Classes and Objects

As we delve deeper into the Python universe, a crucial step in mastering the language is understanding its object-oriented programming (OOP) capabilities. Python's approach to classes and objects not only enhances code reusability but also enables developers to conceive their programs in a more modular, intuitive manner. This chapter introduces the foundational concepts of OOP in Python, demonstrating how to define classes and instantiate objects. We'll explore how these objects can encapsulate data and functionalities, thus becoming the backbone of sophisticated software systems. Special attention will be given to the creation and utility of special methods, which Python uses to integrate objects seamlessly with its language features, and to the concept of inheritance, which promotes code reuse and hierarchy in object-oriented design. By the end of this chapter, you'll have a thorough understanding of how classes and objects operate in Python and why they're pivotal in developing well-structured, efficient code. This knowledge will serve as a cornerstone for more advanced topics in the following chapters, where exception handling, Pythonic code idioms, and interactions with Python's rich ecosystem of libraries and frameworks are discussed.

Object-Oriented Programming Concepts

Object-oriented programming (OOP) stands as a pivotal pillar in the realm of Python advanced programming. It is a programming paradigm based on the concept of "objects", which can contain data, in the form of attributes, and code, in the form of methods. OOP focuses on decomposing a problem into manageable pieces by modeling tangible entities in the software domain.

The cornerstone of OOP in Python is the class. A class acts as a blueprint for creating objects (instances), encapsulating data for the object and methods to operate on that data. This approach to programming simplifies complex code bases, making them more modular, scalable, and reusable.

Inheritance is another fundamental aspect of OOP, allowing new classes to adopt attributes and methods of existing classes. This leads to a hierarchical organization of classes and the reuse of common logic, while still providing the flexibility to introduce unique behaviors in the derived classes. In Python, inheritance is straightforward, enabling single and multiple inheritance patterns that empower developers to build sophisticated relationships between classes.

Polymorphism, derived from Greek meaning "many shapes," refers to the ability of different classes to be treated as instances of the same class through a shared interface. This is often achieved through method overriding, where a method in a derived class has the same name but performs a different function than a method in its base class. Polymorphism in Python enriches the flexibility and dynamism of code, allowing functions to operate on objects of different classes as long as they adhere to a common protocol.

Encapsulation is another core OOP principle, enabling objects to hide their internal state and requiring that outside entities interact with them through an exposed interface. This promotes code safety and reduces complexity, making maintenance and development more manageable. In Python, encapsulation is not enforced as strictly as in some other languages; however, naming conventions (using an underscore prefix) provide a clear indication of protected and private attributes.

The concept of composition over inheritance suggests favoring composition, the inclusion of objects within other objects, to achieve code reuse and flexibility. Python's dynamic nature and first-class functions allow for elegant compositional designs, which can often be more modular and easier to understand than deep inheritance hierarchies.

Dynamic binding and duck typing are features of Python that allow it to embody OOP principles with great flexibility. Dynamic binding refers to the runtime association of a method to a class object, and duck typing allows an object to be used in any context, provided it has the right methods and attributes, regardless of its class. This permits a highly dynamic and flexible coding style, perfectly aligning with the polymorphic nature of Python.

Abstract base classes (ABCs) in Python provide a mechanism for defining interfaces when developing large-scale applications. Through the **abc** module, developers can define methods that must be implemented by subclasses, enforcing a contract and reducing the possibilities of errors.

Another merit of OOP is its support for handling complexity. By organizing code into classes and objects, developers can tackle complex software design challenges more effectively. This modularity allows for focusing on one part of the system at a time and promotes code reuse across projects.

Python enhances OOP with its own set of functionalities like decorators, which can augment the behavior of methods and classes, and metaclasses, which allow for customizing class creation. These features provide powerful tools for developers, enabling sophisticated design patterns and idioms within the Python ecosystem.

Understanding OOP concepts in Python is crucial for developers aiming to build scalable and efficient applications. The transition from procedural to object-oriented programming can be enlightening, revealing new strategies to simplify the design and implementation of complex systems.

When used appropriately, OOP can significantly improve the readability and maintainability of code. It facilitates a deeper understanding of the problem domain and promotes a more natural and intuitive way of thinking about solutions. Object-oriented programs often mirror the real-world scenario they are trying to represent, making them more understandable and easier to explain to non-programmers.

However, it's important to recognize that OOP is not a silver bullet. The added layer of abstraction can introduce overhead and sometimes lead to unnecessary complexity. Therefore, it's essential to strike a balance between the use of OOP principles and other programming paradigms like functional programming, which Python also supports. The ultimate choice depends on the specific requirements and constraints of the project at hand.

In summary, object-oriented programming in Python offers a robust set of concepts and mechanisms to organize and structure code in a way that is reusable, maintainable, and scalable. By embracing the principles of classes and objects, inheritance, polymorphism, encapsulation, and composition, Python developers can tackle a broad spectrum of software development challenges, making OOP a cornerstone of professional Python programming.

Defining Classes and Creating Objects

In the evolution of learning Python, understanding classes and objects is a pivotal step. This chapter transition from foundational concepts to the object-oriented nature of Python. Object-oriented programming (OOP) provides a structure for code that is more reusable and easier to maintain. To embark on this journey, one must first grasp the basics of defining classes and creating objects.

A class in Python serves as a blueprint for creating objects. Objects are instances of classes, possessing their unique attributes and behaviors as defined by their class. This paradigm allows programmers to model real-world entities within their code, creating a more intuitive design process. Let's begin by defining a simple class.

To define a class in Python, use the keyword *class*, followed by the class name and a colon. The naming convention for classes is to start with an uppercase letter, with the rest of the name in lowercase if it's a single word, or in CamelCase for multiple words. For instance, **class Dog:** defines a new class named Dog.

Within a class, one can define methods and attributes. Methods are functions that belong to a class, and attributes are variables. Both define the behavior and properties of objects created from the class. For example, our Dog class could have a method **bark** and an attribute **age**.

Creating an object, or an instance of a class, is straightforward. Simply call the class as if it were a function, and you'll get an object out of it. For example, **my_dog = Dog()** creates a new Dog object and assigns it to the variable **my_dog**.

But how do we specify attributes like age for our Dog objects? This is where the *__init__* method comes in. The *__init__* method is a special method that Python calls when a new object is created. It's typically used to initialize attributes. For example, we can define *__init__* in our Dog class to accept an age parameter and assign it to the object's **age** attribute.

Encapsulation is another key concept in OOP, referring to the bundling of data with the methods that operate on that data, or the restriction of direct access to some of the object's components. Python doesn't have private variables like some other languages, but it is a convention to prefix a name with an underscore (_) to indicate that it is intended for internal use only.

Inheritance is a way to create a new class using details of an existing class without modifying it. The new class is called a derived (or child) class and the one from which it inherits is called the base (or parent) class. Python allows for inheritance, which will be covered in detail in the next section.

Polymorphism is another OOP concept that allows for methods to do different things based on the object it is called on. This is achieved through method overriding. Python implements polymorphism by default, as Python is more flexible with types.

Instances of a class are created by calling the class using its name followed by parentheses. If the *__init__* method is defined, its parameters other than **self** must be passed. The **self** parameter in the method definition is a reference to the instance of the class, and it's how attributes and other methods are accessed.

You can add as many methods to a class as you need. An important part of working in an object-oriented way is thinking about how your objects interact with one another. This involves methods that work internally within an object but also how objects can use each other's methods and attributes.

Python also supports class attributes, which are shared across all instances of a class. They are defined within the class but outside any methods. Class attributes are useful for constants related to the class or for tracking data across all instances.

Understanding the relationship between classes (the blueprint) and objects (the instances created from the class) is critical. A well-defined class can encapsulate complex behavior and state, allowing the rest of your code to interact with objects in a clear and predictable way.

To summarize, defining classes and creating objects are central to Python's approach to OOP. Classes provide the templates for objects, encapsulating attributes and behaviors. By mastering these concepts, developers can build more modular, scalable, and maintainable applications. The transformation from procedural to object-oriented programming not only improves the structure of code but also enhances its real-world applicability.

As we move forward, remember that Python's philosophy encourages readability and simplicity. These principles are evident in its approach to OOP, making it a powerful tool for both novice and experienced programmers. The subsequent sections will delve into special methods that further enrich class definitions and inheritance, which extends the functionality of existing classes.

Special Methods and Inheritance

Transitioning into the more refined aspects of Python, we delve into special methods and inheritance, critical concepts for anyone looking to master Python's object-oriented programming features. Special methods allow Python classes to implement and interact with built-in Python operations. These methods are identifiable by their double underscores before and after the method name, for example, **__init__** or **__str__**.

Starting with the **__init__** method, commonly known as the constructor in other programming languages, it's used to initialize new objects from a class. It's the method that allows us to pass initial values to our object's attributes. However, **__init__** is just the tip of the iceberg. Let's say we want to define how two objects of our class should be added together. This is where the **__add__** special method comes into play, enabling us to use the + operator with our objects in a meaningful way.

Similarly, the __**str**__ method defines what happens when we call the built-in **str()** function on an instance of our class, allowing us to return a user-friendly string representation of our object. This is especially useful for debugging and logging purposes when we need a clear text representation of our object's state.

Moving on to inheritance, another cornerstone of object-oriented programming, it permits us to create a hierarchy of classes. A 'subclass' can inherit methods and attributes from a 'superclass', facilitating code reuse and the creation of more complex relationships between objects. This mechanism allows for extending the functionality of existing code without modifying it, adhering to the "Open/Closed" principle.

Python supports multiple inheritance as well, a concept where a class can inherit behaviors and characteristics from more than one parent class. This feature offers a tremendous amount of flexibility but requires careful design to avoid the pitfalls associated with it, such as the notorious "diamond problem". Python's method resolution order (MRO) and the **super()** function resolve these complexities, ensuring a clear and linear way to call superclass methods.

One of the essential benefits of inheritance is polymorphism. It allows methods defined in a subclass to have the same name as methods in the superclass but to behave differently. For instance, if we have a method named **draw()** in a class named **Shape**, a subclass named **Circle** could implement **draw()** to draw a circle, while a **Square** subclass might implement it to draw a square.

Ideally, when designing classes for inheritance, we need to ensure that they adhere to the Liskov Substitution Principle. This principle dictates that objects of a superclass shall be replaceable with objects of a subclass without affecting the correctness of the program. It emphasizes the importance of designing subclasses that can stand in for their superclasses.

Overriding methods in subclasses allows for custom behavior while retaining the interface of the superclass. This is a powerful feature that, when combined with the use of **super()**, enables subclasses to enhance or modify the behavior of superclass methods in a controlled and mindful manner.

Mixins are a design pattern that can be implemented via multiple inheritance in Python. They are a sort of class that is intended to provide an additional capability or enhancement to a class without being part of the primary inheritance chain. For example, a **JsonMixin** might provide a method to serialize an object to JSON, adding this capability to any class that requires it without needing to inherit from a specific parent class.

Understanding the concept of abstract base classes (ABCs) is also crucial. In Python, ABCs define a set of methods that must be created within any subclass implementations. By using the **abc** module, you can create classes that cannot be instantiated themselves but serve as a blueprint for subclasses. This ensures that certain methods are always present in the class hierarchies derived from these abstract classes.

The journey through special methods and inheritance provides a solid understanding of how to create versatile and reusable object-oriented code in Python. By grasively applying these concepts, you can write code that is both efficient and easy to maintain, moving closer to mastering Python's full potential.

As we wrap up this section, remember that the power of special methods and inheritance lies in their ability to abstract complexity and encapsulate functionality. Proper use of these features can elevate your Python code, making it more robust, scalable, and, importantly, Pythonic.

With the foundational knowledge of special methods and inheritance, you are well-equipped to delve into more specialized

Python features, such as descriptor classes, metaclasses, and the dynamic creation of classes. These advanced topics, while beyond the scope of this section, build upon the principles covered here and open the door to even deeper levels of Python programming mastery.

Last but not least, always keep in mind the principle of "composition over inheritance." While inheritance is a powerful tool, it's not always the best solution. Often, composing classes by including them as attributes in other classes can provide more flexibility and reduce complexity. This approach promotes loose coupling and high cohesion, guiding principles for designing maintainable and scalable software.

Through the intelligent application of special methods and inheritance, you'll find your Python programs not only work well but also integrate seamlessly with the Python ecosystem. This knowledge is a stepping stone to becoming not just a Python programmer, but a Pythonic programmer.

Chapter 5: Exception Handling in Python

As our journey through Python progresses, we find that understanding and managing unexpected events in our code is crucial for building robust applications. Exception handling in Python is not just about preventing your programs from crashing unexpectedly; it's a way to ensure they behave predictably under all circumstances, including user error, resource constraints, or external system failures. Python provides a flexible framework for intercepting errors, diagnosing issues, and responding appropriately, which is critical for both new and experienced developers aiming to create professional-grade software.

In this chapter, we dive into the mechanisms Python offers for identifying and handling exceptions. We begin by exploring some of the most common exceptions you might encounter, such as **IndexError**, **KeyError**, **TypeError**, and **ValueError**. Understanding these exceptions will help you anticipate and plan for potential issues in your codebase. Next, we delve into the structure and use of **try-except** blocks, Python's primary tool for catching and managing exceptions. We'll cover how to catch specific exceptions, how to use **else** and **finally** clauses for clean-up actions, and how exceptions can be chained or re-raised to provide more context to the caller.

Moreover, we'll explore the importance of raising exceptions intentionally in your code. Doing so can signal to other parts of your application that something has gone wrong, providing a clear protocol for error reporting and handling. We will discuss best practices for defining and using custom exception classes to more precisely indicate the nature of errors in your programs. By the end of this chapter, you'll be equipped with the knowledge to use Python's exception handling features effectively, improving the reliability and usability of your software.

Common Exceptions

In Python, as in any programming language, errors and exceptions are an unavoidable part of writing code. Understanding common exceptions is crucial for debugging and writing robust, error-handled code. This chapter details some of the most frequent exceptions you might encounter, their causes, and how to handle them gracefully.

First and foremost, the *SyntaxError* occurs when Python encounters incorrect code that it cannot parse. This could be due to typographical errors, such as missing colons, parentheses, or incorrect indentation, which are crucial in Python's syntax. It's one of the first exceptions beginners encounter, and improving your attention to code structure often resolves it.

An *IndentationError* is a specific type of SyntaxError. Python uses indentation to define code blocks, unlike many other languages that use braces. An incorrect indent can lead to this error and the solution is often as simple as checking that your blocks are properly aligned.

The *NameError* happens when Python code attempts to use a name that has not been defined. This could be due to misspelling a variable name or trying to use a variable before it is declared. It's a reminder of Python's case-sensitivity and the importance of defining your variables before use.

An *IndexError* is thrown when you try to access an index out of the range of a list or string. This often happens in loops or when accessing elements without verifying the collection's size. It's a good practice to always check the length of a collection before attempting to access its elements by index.

Related to **IndexError**, the *KeyError* occurs when a dictionary does not have a specified key. Dictionaries in Python are accessed via keys, and attempting to retrieve a non-existent key will throw this exception. To avoid this, you can use the **get()** method of dictionaries, which returns **None** (or a default value you can specify) instead of throwing an error.

The *TypeError* occurs when an operation or function is applied to an object of an inappropriate type. This can happen when you try to concatenate a string with a number, for example. The solution often involves converting data types or using more appropriate operations that match the data types involved.

A *ValueError* is raised when a function receives an argument with the right type but an inappropriate value. This could occur if you're trying to find the square root of a negative number or converting a string that does not represent a number to an integer. Careful data validation is the key to avoiding this type of exception.

The *AttributeError* is triggered when an attribute reference or assignment fails. If you attempt to use a method or attribute that doesn't exist on an object, Python will raise this exception. This is common when dealing with external libraries and misunderstanding their APIs. It's often remedied by reviewing the object's documentation or using the built-in **dir()** function to inspect available methods and attributes.

Handling file operations can lead to several exceptions, such as the *FileNotFoundError* when attempting to open a file that does not exist. This can be avoided by checking for a file's existence with the **os.path.exists()** method before attempting to open it. Other file-related exceptions include *PermissionError* and *IOError*, which can occur when you don't have the necessary permissions to access the file or when an I/O operation fails, respectively.

Network programming introduces the *ConnectionError*, which is a base class for exceptions related to network connections. Its subclasses, like *ConnectionResetError*, are specific to situations where connections are reset, timed out, or otherwise unexpectedly closed. In network programming, handling these exceptions involves retrying operations or gracefully informing the user about the connection issue.

When working with numerical operations, the *ZeroDivisionError* is a common exception that occurs when a division or modulo operation is attempted with zero as the divisor. This is prevented by validating inputs to ensure they are not zero before performing such operations.

The *OverflowError* and *MemoryError* are less common but can occur in numerical computations. The former happens when a calculation exceeds the limit of a numeric type, and the latter when your program runs out of memory. These are indicative of issues that might require optimizing your code or data structures.

Lastly, the *StopIteration* exception signals that an iterator has no more values to provide, commonly encountered in for loops and generator functions. Understanding this exception is crucial when creating custom iterators or working extensively with generators and iterables.

In conclusion, while this list of common exceptions in Python is non-exhaustive, being familiar with them and understanding how to address their underlying causes can greatly enhance your debugging skills and code quality. With practice, you'll become adept at not only fixing these errors but preventing them from occurring in the first place. Remember, exception handling is not about avoiding errors entirely but about anticipating and gracefully managing the unexpected.

Try-Except Blocks

Error handling is an essential aspect of writing robust Python programs. Among the various mechanisms Python provides for handling errors, the try-except block is perhaps the most notable and widely used. This block allows programmers to anticipate potential errors and manage them effectively, thus ensuring that the program can handle unexpected inputs or situations without crashing.

The basic structure of a try-except block is straightforward. A "try" clause is written, containing the code that might generate an exception, followed by one or more "except" clauses which specify how Python should respond to specific exceptions. This structure enables the programmer to catch and handle errors, providing an opportunity to recover from the error or fail gracefully, potentially logging the problem for future reference.

Using try-except blocks promotes the writing of safer code. In an environment where data integrity and program stability are paramount, being able to predict and control the behavior of your software under adverse conditions is invaluable. It's not merely about preventing your program from crashing - it's also about providing meaningful feedback to the user and ensuring that the program can continue to operate effectively even when encountering unexpected circumstances.

One of the key benefits of using try-except blocks is the ability to manage multiple exception types. Python allows you to catch different exceptions separately and handle them according to their nature. This specificity in error handling makes your code more readable and helps with debugging, as it's clearer what types of errors you're expecting in each section of your code.

However, it's important not to overuse try-except blocks. They should not be employed to avoid dealing with known errors or to make up for poor coding practices. Using exception handling to control the flow of your program, rather than as a means to deal with truly exceptional conditions, can lead to code that's hard to understand and maintain.

An advanced feature of try-except blocks is the "else" clause. This clause can be added after the last except block to specify a block of code to be executed if no exceptions were raised. The else clause helps improve code clarity by separating the successful path of the code from the error handling sections.

Moreover, the "finally" clause can be used alongside or independently of except blocks. It defines a block of code that will be executed no matter what - whether an exception is raised or not. This is particularly useful for resource management tasks, such as closing file streams or network connections in a guaranteed manner, ensuring that resources are not left open or in an undefined state.

It's worth noting that the try-except block can also be nested within other try-except blocks. This allows for a more granular control of exception handling, where an inner block handles more specific exceptions that could occur in a subset of the try block's code, while outer blocks handle more general exceptions.

When dealing with standard library functions or third-party libraries, it becomes crucial to understand what types of exceptions can be raised by these external sources. This knowledge allows you to write effective try-except blocks that can handle those specific exceptions, improving the reliability and user experience of your program.

Practicing the art of exception handling can greatly improve your debugging skills. By forcing you to anticipate potential errors, it enables you to think more critically about the paths your code can take and the points at which it may fail. This proactive approach to problem-solving is beneficial not only for error handling but for the development of programming skills in general.

Another consideration when using try-except blocks is performance. While it's generally not advisable to use these blocks for flow control, there can be performance implications in Python when exceptions are raised in a large quantity. However, in most practical applications, the impact is negligible compared to the benefits of writing safe and robust code.

Ultimately, the goal of using try-except blocks is to increase the resilience of your software. By anticipating and managing exceptions effectively, you can ensure that your programs are more reliable and provide a better user experience. Whether it's gracefully handling a failed database connection or dealing with incorrect input formats, exception handling is a powerful tool in any Python programmer's toolkit.

While the mechanics of try-except blocks are relatively simple, mastering their effective use requires practice and a deep understanding of the types of exceptions your code can encounter. With time and experience, you'll find that exception handling not only makes your code more robust but also deepens your understanding of Python's execution model.

In conclusion, try-except blocks are a fundamental feature of Python programming that enable developers to write safer, more reliable code. By understanding and utilizing this feature effectively, you can greatly enhance the resilience and usability of your Python applications. As you continue on your journey as a Python programmer, integrating sophisticated exception handling strategies into your coding practice will undoubtedly be a key factor in your success.

Raising Exceptions

In programming, ensuring the correctness, stability, and security of your code is paramount. Exception handling serves as a safety net for when things go wrong. Within the realm of Python, raising exceptions is a pivotal technique that developers can use to handle errors and exceptional cases proactively. This section explores the mechanism of raising exceptions, why it's needed, and how it can be employed effectively in Python programs.

At its core, an exception is an event that disrupts the normal flow of a program's execution. When Python encounters an unexpected situation, it raises an exception. Developers, however, are not just passive recipients of these system-raised exceptions. The Python language provides the *raise* keyword to allow programmers to trigger exceptions manually. This can be particularly useful for enforcing constraints, validating input, or signaling that certain conditions have later become impossible or erroneous.

To raise an exception in Python, simply use the *raise* statement followed by an instance of the exception class you aim to trigger. For example, raising a **ValueError** when an incorrect value is received can guide users or calling functions towards necessary corrective actions. The statement looks like: **raise ValueError("This is a message explaining the error.")**

The beauty of raising exceptions lies in its ability to gracefully interrupt program execution, allowing control to jump to a corresponding exception handler. This mechanism facilitates a structured and predictable way to handle errors and special conditions without cluttering the code with excessive error checks and conditional logic.

It's important to distinguish between system-defined and user-defined exceptions. While Python comes with a broad range of built-in exceptions that cater to many common error conditions, it also allows the creation of custom exceptions. By extending the base Exception class, developers can craft meaningful, readable exceptions tailored to their specific application's needs.

When raising exceptions, it's crucial to provide insightful messages that can aid in quickly pinpointing what went wrong. A well-crafted error message not only reduces debugging time but also enhances the maintainability of your code. This is especially true when developing libraries or frameworks where the user of your code might not have immediate visibility into the internals.

Another essential aspect to consider is when to raise an exception. Overuse of raising exceptions can make a program chaotic and difficult to follow, whereas underusing it can leave your program vulnerable to silent failures. Striking a balance is key. It's generally advisable to raise exceptions in situations where a function cannot complete its defined task due to improper inputs or an unsatisfied precondition.

Exception chains provide context to the handling of multiple, related exceptions by preserving the original traceback. This is achieved using the *from* keyword in a raise statement. For example, when you catch an exception but need to raise another exception that's directly related, you can chain them using **raise NewException() from original_exception** to preserve the original context. This chaining helps in debugging by providing a clearer causal relationship between exceptions.

Effective exception handling strategies often involve creating a hierarchy of exceptions in larger projects. This organization allows you to capture exceptions at different levels of specificity. Broad, generic exceptions can be caught at the top level of your program, while more specific exceptions can be handled at the component or module level.

Handling raised exceptions involves wrapping code blocks that may throw exceptions in try-except blocks. When an exception is raised, Python looks for the nearest enclosing try-except block that can handle the exception by type. If no suitable handler is found in the current function, the exception propagates up the call stack, allowing higher levels of the program an opportunity to respond.

Finally, it's worth mentioning the importance of cleaning up after exceptions. The *finally* block in Python's try-except structure ensures that cleanup code is executed regardless of whether an exception was raised or not. This is ideal for releasing external resources like files or network connections, making your code more robust and error-resistant.

In summary, raising exceptions in Python is a powerful feature that, when used judiciously, can significantly enhance the reliability and clarity of your code. By understanding when and how to raise exceptions, you can write code that's not only robust but also easier to debug and maintain. As you grow more experienced in Python programming, you'll come to appreciate the nuance and art of effectively managing exceptions in your projects.

As we continue to explore Python's exception handling capabilities, keep in mind that mastering the art of raising and handling exceptions is a key step towards writing clean, professional, and maintainable Python code. Whether you're a beginner or an advanced Python programmer, developing a deep understanding of exception handling will undoubtedly serve you well in your coding endeavors.

Chapter 6: Pythonic Code and Best Practices

As we transition from understanding Python's core concepts and delving into exception handling, a crucial chapter awaits that could significantly enhance the way we write and understand Python code. "Pythonic Code and Best Practices" is not just a series of rules to follow; it's an ethos that elevates your coding skills from simply writing scripts that work to crafting code that speaks volumes in terms of readability, efficiency, and elegance. This chapter is dedicated to unraveling what it means to write Pythonic code, a term that you'll often hear among seasoned developers. It's about adhering to the Python Enhancement Proposal (PEP 8), which details the style guidelines for Python, ensuring code is not just functional but also clean and maintainable. We'll explore strategies for writing readable Python code that communicates its intent clearly, not just to machines, but more importantly, to humans who may interact with it down the line. Moreover, we'll delve into optimization techniques, helping you understand how to make your code more efficient and performant without sacrificing readability. By the end of this chapter, you'll have a solid grasp of best practices that will guide you in your Python journey, making your code not just work but shine.

Writing Readable Python Code

One essential aspect that often gets overlooked by beginners yet is profoundly respected within the Python community is the readability of code. Python's design philosophy emphasizes simplicity and readability which can significantly influence the maintenance and scalability of applications. As developers progress in their Python journey, they come to realize the importance of writing code that not just works, but is also understandable to others and their future selves.

Readability comes from a combination of several factors, including naming conventions, code structure, and the use of whitespace. Python's adherence to simplicity allows for the creation of powerful functionalities with minimal code, but this advantage can lead to overly dense and unintelligible code blocks if not managed properly. It's critical to balance Pythonic conciseness with clarity.

Adopting meaningful variable names is the first step toward readable code. Variables should be named in a way that reflects their purpose or the data they hold. Using abstract names like 'x' or 'data' does little to illuminate their function within the program. A variable name like 'student_grades' immediately tells us what kind of data it might contain, enhancing our understanding of the code block at a glance.

Similarly, naming conventions for functions and classes should follow a descriptive approach. Function names should typically start with a verb, suggesting the action they perform. For example, 'calculate_average_score' is preferable to 'calc_avg,' as it is much explicit about what the function does. Python's official style guide, PEP 8, provides extensive recommendations for naming and other stylistic choices that promote readability.

The structure of the code also contributes significantly to its readability. Python's use of indentation to define block scopes—such as in if statements, loops, and function definitions—is a boon for readability, making the code's structure visually apparent. However, developers must avoid deeply nested structures, as they can complicate understanding. It's often better to refactor complex blocks into functions or loops to maintain depth that is easy to follow.

Comments and docstrings play a vital role in making code more readable. While the code itself should be as self-explanatory as possible, comments can provide much-needed context or explain the rationale behind certain decisions. Docstrings, placed at the beginning of modules, classes, and functions, offer a more formal way to document the purpose and usage of the code block they describe.

Effective use of whitespace is another tool in the Python programmer's kit for enhancing readability. Python's syntax naturally incorporates whitespace for block delineation, but additional spaces and blank lines can be used to separate logical sections of code, making them easier to scan and comprehend at a glance.

Choosing the right data structures is not just a matter of performance or capability, but also of readability. Python offers a variety of built-in data structures, such as lists, dictionaries, tuples, and sets, each with its unique advantages. Selecting the appropriate type for the job can make the code more intuitive and straightforward. For instance, dictionaries are excellent for pairing related data, making the code that utilizes them for such purposes more readable than if lists or tuples were used incorrectly.

Python's extensive standard library is another resource that, when leveraged properly, can significantly improve the readability of your code. By utilizing well-documented and widely understood modules and functions, developers can avoid reinventing the wheel, instead focusing on the unique aspects of their project. This not only saves time but also ensures that the codebase remains accessible to other Python developers familiar with these standard solutions.

Refactoring is the process of restructuring existing code without changing its behavior to improve its internal structure. Regularly refactoring code to simplify complex functions, reduce redundancy, and apply design patterns can greatly enhance readability and maintainability. It's a practice that demands a deep understanding of

Python and its idioms but pays dividends by making the code more elegant and easier to work with in the long run.

Testing, surprisingly, can also impact the readability of your code. Well-written tests serve as live documentation for your codebase, illustrating usage and expected behavior. They provide a form of assurance that your refactoring and optimization efforts haven't altered the intended functionality, encouraging more aggressive cleanup and simplification efforts.

Error handling, when done correctly, can make a significant difference in code readability. Python's approach to exceptions encourages the use of try-except blocks to manage potential errors. A clear, concise handling of exceptions not only prevents your program from crashing but also makes it clearer to other developers how the program deals with unexpected inputs or states.

Lastly, embracing Python's philosophy of "There should be one--and preferably only one --obvious way to do it" can drastically improve code readability. This philosophy encourages consistency in problem-solving approaches within the Python community. By adhering to well-established patterns and idioms, developers ensure that their solutions are straightforward for others to understand and follow.

In conclusion, writing readable Python code is a multifaceted discipline that combines naming conventions, structure, documentation, and the judicious use of Python's features. It is a skill that developers refine over time, learning not just from their own experiences but also from engaging with the community and studying other codebases. By prioritizing readability, developers can create more maintainable, understandable, and ultimately successful Python projects.

The pursuit of readability in Python is not just about writing code that computers can execute. It's about writing code that humans can easily read, understand, and modify. As you continue to grow as a Python developer, remember that the clarity of your code is as important as its correctness. The practices and principles discussed in this section are intended to guide you toward writing Python code that excels in both respects.

Python Style Guide (PEP 8)

Adhering to a style guide is crucial for maintaining the readability and maintainability of your code, especially when it comes to collaborative projects. The Python Enhancement Proposal 8, commonly known as PEP 8, is the de facto coding standard for writing Python code. It covers a range of topics from naming conventions to indentation, ensuring that Python code is not only functional but also clean and consistent.

One foundational aspect of PEP 8 is its emphasis on readability. Python's core philosophy revolves around the significance of code readability, and PEP 8 reinforces this by providing explicit guidelines on how to format Python code. These guidelines help in making your code visually appealing and easier to read, which, in turn, makes it easier to understand and maintain over time.

Naming conventions play a pivotal role in PEP 8, distinguishing between different types of identifiers. Variables and function names should use lowercase with underscores to improve readability, for example, **my_variable** or **calculate_value**. Classes, on the other hand, should follow the CapWords convention, where each word starts with a capital letter, without underscores, such as **MyClass**. Consistent naming makes your code intuitive to navigate and understand for both you and others who might work with your code in the future.

Indentation is another critical element outlined in PEP 8. Python uses indentation to define code blocks, and PEP 8 specifies using 4 spaces per indentation level. This standardization ensures that code structure is clearly defined across different environments and editors, aiding both readability and portability.

Whitespace is yet another tool underlined by PEP 8 for readability enhancement. Strategic use of whitespace can make complex expressions more manageable and can delineate logical sections of code. However, it's crucial to avoid excessive whitespace, such as inside parentheses, brackets, or braces, and between trailing commas and closing identifiers. The correct use of whitespace contributes to the visual clarity and overall aesthetics of your code.

PEP 8 also addresses the optimal line length for Python code. It recommends limiting lines to 79 characters to facilitate reading code on smaller displays and to allow for side-by-side comparisons in code reviews. While modern displays can accommodate much longer lines, adhering to this guideline ensures that your code is easily accessible across various devices and situations.

Comments are a valuable part of any codebase, and PEP 8 provides specific recommendations for writing them. Comments should always be up-to-date with the code and written in full sentences. The goal of a comment is to clarify the purpose and functionality of the associated code; thus, clarity and brevity are paramount. In-line comments should be used sparingly and must be separated by at least two spaces from the statement.

In terms of structuring imports, PEP 8 suggests a particular order: standard library imports first, followed by third-party imports, and then local application/library specific imports. Each section should be separated by blank lines. This separation and ordering can help in quickly identifying dependencies and understanding the relationships between various components of the code.

The document also delves into the realm of exceptions, providing guidance on how to handle them effectively. For instance, it recommends using explicit exception types in **try/except** blocks rather than bare except clauses. This specificity helps in catching exactly the intended errors and makes the code's error handling path clearer to future readers.

While PEP 8 serves as an extensive guide to writing clean Python code, it's important to treat it as a guideline rather than a strict rulebook. The ultimate goal is to enhance code readability and maintainability. There may be instances where deviating from a particular recommendation might make sense, especially if adhering to it would result in less readable or less efficient code. Thus, exercising judgment and considering the context is key when applying PEP 8 guidelines.

For teams and projects, adopting PEP 8 in its entirety or a customized subset can significantly improve code quality. It facilitates smoother collaboration, eases the onboarding process for new team members, and can lead to more efficient and effective code reviews.

Tools like **flake8** and **pylint** can assist in enforcing PEP 8 standards across your projects. These tools not only check your code for stylistic deviations but also help in identifying potential programming errors, further bolstering code quality. Integrating these tools into your development process can make adherence to PEP 8 both efficient and systematic.

The Python community, being vast and active, continually discusses and updates the guidelines in PEP 8 to reflect the evolving best practices in software development. Therefore, staying abreast of these updates is essential for keeping your Python coding skills sharp and relevant.

To sum up, the Python Style Guide (PEP 8) is a cornerstone of Python programming, advocating for readability, consistency, and quality in coding practices. By embracing PEP 8, developers ensure that their code is accessible, maintainable, and in harmony with the broader Python community's norms. As you continue your journey in Python programming, integrating PEP 8 guidelines into your coding practices can lead to significant improvements in both your individual and collaborative coding endeavors.

Optimization Techniques

When delving into Pythonic code and best practices, understanding and applying optimization techniques is critical for developing efficient and scalable Python applications. Optimization in Python can span several dimensions, from how the code is written to how it's executed. This section will explore several avenues through which Python code can be optimized for better performance and readability.

One fundamental aspect of writing optimized Python code is understanding the nuances of Python's execution model. Python is an interpreted language, meaning that the Python interpreter reads and executes the code line by line. This model can lead to slower execution times compared to compiled languages. However, Python offers several tools and modules, such as PyPy, a just-in-time compiler, that can significantly speed up execution times for Python code.

Another crucial optimization technique involves efficient use of data structures. Python provides a variety of built-in data structures, such as lists, dictionaries, and sets, each with its unique performance characteristics. For instance, using a dictionary for lookups can be much faster than searching through a list, thanks to the underlying hash table implementation. Understanding when and how to use these data structures can greatly affect the performance of a Python program.

Algorithm optimization is an additional area where performance gains can be realized. Simple changes, such as avoiding unnecessary calculations within loops or choosing the most efficient algorithm for a given task, can yield significant improvements. Python's standard library includes the *algorithm* module, which contains a collection of efficient algorithms for tasks like sorting and searching, which developers should leverage whenever possible.

Memory usage is another critical consideration for optimization. Python's memory model can be opaque, leading to inefficient memory use without careful coding. Techniques such as using generators instead of lists for large datasets can dramatically reduce memory footprint. Moreover, Python's garbage collector, which cleans up unused objects, can sometimes be a source of performance overhead, so managing object lifecycle carefully can improve memory usage and speed.

Profiling is an indispensable tool in the optimization arsenal. Profiling allows developers to identify bottlenecks in their code - the sections that are taking the most time or consuming the most memory. Python provides several profiling tools, such as cProfile and memory_profiler, which can help developers understand their code's performance characteristics deeply.

Concurrency and parallelism offer significant opportunities for optimizing Python applications, especially those that are I/O bound or can leverage multiple CPU cores. Python's *threading* and *multiprocessing* modules enable developers to write code that executes concurrently or in parallel, making efficient use of system resources. Furthermore, the *asyncio* library provides support for writing asynchronous I/O operations, which is especially beneficial for IO-bound and network applications.

Caching is a widely used technique to enhance the performance of applications by storing the results of expensive function calls and reusing those results when the same inputs occur again. Python offers *functools.lru_cache*, a decorator that implements a least recently used (LRU) cache which can significantly speed up applications with negligible effort from the developer.

Using compiled extensions is another path to optimization. Python allows for integrating C or C++ extensions, offering a bridge between the ease of Python and the speed of compiled languages. Libraries such as Cython allow Python code to be compiled into C, gaining significant speed advantages.

Writing vectorized operations using libraries like NumPy can also lead to substantial performance improvements. Such operations are performed "at once" on an entire set of data rather than through slow Python loops, exploiting the underlying optimizations and parallelisms of those libraries.

Database interactions can often be a bottleneck in applications. Optimizing database queries and access patterns can significantly impact performance. Techniques include indexing, query optimization, and using connection pools. Python's ORMs (Object-Relational Mappers) and database libraries offer features and configurations tailored towards efficiency.

Finally, maintaining an optimization mindset throughout the development process is crucial. Premature optimization is to be avoided; focus on readability and correctness first, and use profiling to guide optimization efforts. This approach ensures that optimization efforts are both effective and maintainable.

While optimization in Python covers a broad array of techniques and considerations, starting with a strong foundation in Pythonic code and best practices sets the stage for effective optimization. Tools, libraries, and profilers available in the Python ecosystem provide developers with a robust toolkit for enhancing the performance and scalability of their applications, ensuring that Python remains a versatile choice for a wide range of programming needs.

In conclusion, optimization is not a one-time task but a continuous process of refinement and improvement. By leveraging Python's rich ecosystem and observing best practices for clean and efficient code, developers can write applications that are not only correct and readable but also performant and scalable. As we move forward, we'll dive into more specific libraries and frameworks that bring additional performance enhancements and capabilities to Python developers.

Chapter 7: Python Libraries and Frameworks Overview

Embarking on a detailed exploration of Python's extensive toolkit, this chapter serves as a comprehensive guide to the rich ecosystem of libraries and frameworks that elevate Python from a simple scripting language to a powerhouse tool across various domains. From the standard library, which is Python's extensive suite of pre-packaged functionality, to the vibrant selection of third-party libraries that cater to specialized needs in data science, web development, machine learning, and beyond, readers are introduced to the tools that can significantly streamline coding efforts and enhance program functionality. Notably highlighted are Django and Flask, two of the most prominent web frameworks that empower developers to build robust, scalable web applications with fewer lines of code. This overview serves not only to familiarize programmers with the wealth of resources at their disposal but also to illustrate how these libraries and frameworks can be seamlessly integrated into projects. The intent is to provide a solid foundation on which one can build, whether the goal is professional development, academic pursuits, or personal hobby projects. As we proceed, we'll delve deeper into each category, beginning with the standard library highlights, moving through popular third-party libraries, and exploring the intricacies of web frameworks like Django and Flask, ensuring readers have a well-rounded understanding of Python's capabilities.

Standard Library Highlights

The Python standard library is a vast treasure trove of modules and packages that support a wide range of programming tasks. From handling dates and times to accessing the file system, the standard library provides robust solutions that are efficient, reliable, and secure. In this section, we delve into some of the key highlights of the Python standard library, shedding light on the power and flexibility that Python offers straight out of the box.

Firstly, it's crucial to understand that the Python standard library is built-in; there's no need for additional installations to utilize its features. This aspect is particularly beneficial for beginners, as it simplifies the learning curve and enables novices to tap into advanced functionalities without grappling with package management systems.

One of the most frequently used modules is *sys*, which provides access to some variables used or maintained by the Python interpreter and functions that interact strongly with the interpreter. Through *sys*, programmers can manipulate Python runtime environment, delve into the intricacies of command-line arguments, and handle various environment settings. This module acts as a bridge between the Python environment and the operating system.

Another cornerstone of Python programming is the *os* module, enabling interaction with the operating system. Whether it's navigating through directories, manipulating paths, or managing file permissions, the *os* module offers a portable way of using operating system-dependent functionality. It abstracts the complexities of different OS-specific operations, making code more portable and easier to maintain.

For tasks related to file I/O (Input/Output), the *pathlib* module has transformed the way file paths and operations are handled. Introduced in Python 3.4, *pathlib* provides a more intuitive approach to file system paths with its object-oriented interface. Developers can perform most path manipulations without necessarily converting them into strings, leading to more readable and efficient code.

Date and time manipulation is another area where the standard library shines with the *datetime* module. It supports easy creation and manipulation of dates, times, and intervals. The support for arithmetic operations, formatting, and parsing ensures that handling temporal data is straightforward and hassle-free.

Parsing command-line arguments is streamlined with the *argparse* module, which automates the process of accepting arguments from users, validating them, and converting them into Python data types. It's a powerful tool for creating user-friendly command-line interfaces for scripts and applications.

For network communication, the *socket* module is indispensable, providing a low-level networking interface that supports both traditional TCP/IP and newer protocols. Programmers can use it to implement custom networking protocols or interact with existing servers and services efficiently.

The *json* module offers powerful support for parsing and emitting JSON, a lightweight data interchange format widely used in APIs and web services. Python's *json* module not only simplifies data serialization and deserialization but also promotes interoperability between applications written in Python and those in other languages.

Error handling in Python is facilitated through exceptions, and the *traceback* module provides utilities for working with them effectively. It helps in generating and formatting stack traces, essential for diagnosing errors in applications.

Performing mathematical and random number operations is streamlined with the *math* and *random* modules, respectively. These modules encapsulate a wide range of mathematical functions and algorithms for random number generation, supporting everything from basic arithmetic to complex trigonometry and statistical operations.

Lastly, the *unittest* module deserves a mention for its role in Python's approach to test-driven development. It provides a robust framework for constructing and running tests, ensuring that applications behave as intended before they are deployed or integrated into larger systems.

The Python standard library is an extensive resource that underpins Python's versatility as a programming language. While we've highlighted some of the key modules, the library encompasses much more, covering areas such as compression, multimedia handling, and internet protocols, among others. Exploring the standard library is a journey of discovery, revealing the depth and breadth of Python's capabilities.

In conclusion, the Python standard library is a critical component of the Python programming ecosystem. It equips developers with a comprehensive set of modules and packages that cater to a wide array of programming needs. Understanding and leveraging the standard library can significantly enhance the effectiveness and efficiency of Python code, making it an indispensable resource for developers at all levels.

As you continue with the Python journey, diving deeper into the standard library will reveal more about the language's philosophy—simplicity in design, emphasis on readability, and a strong preference for a "batteries-included" approach. Harnessing the power of the standard library is a stepping stone towards mastering Python and unlocking its full potential in solving real-world problems.

Popular Third-Party Libraries

In the Python ecosystem, third-party libraries play a significant role in extending the language's core functionality, catering to a wide array of applications from web development to data analysis, machine learning, and beyond. These libraries, developed and maintained by the community, offer robust solutions that streamline coding tasks and enhance productivity. This section delves into some of the most popular and widely-used third-party libraries that have become essential tools for Python programmers across various skill levels.

Requests: When it comes to handling HTTP requests in Python, the Requests library is the de facto standard. With its simple and intuitive API, Requests makes it easy to send HTTP/1.1 requests, without the need for manual labor like encoding URLs and form data. It's praised for its elegance and ease of use, turning a complex task into a straightforward one.

NumPy: For numerical computing, NumPy is an indispensable library. It provides support for large, multi-dimensional arrays and matrices, along with a collection of mathematical functions to operate on these data structures. Its performance, due to underlying C and Fortran code, makes data manipulation and analysis both fast and efficient, a reason why it's heavily used in both academia and industry.

Pandas: Building on NumPy, Pandas is a powerhouse for data manipulation and analysis. It introduces dataframes and series, making data cleaning, transformation, and analysis tasks seamless. Pandas excel in handling time-series data, missing data, and aligning data from disparate sources in a way that's intuitive and accessible.

Matplotlib: For data visualization, Matplotlib is the foundational library. It allows for the creation of static, animated, and interactive visualizations in Python. Matplotlib is highly customizable and works well with NumPy and Pandas, making it a go-to for plotting data with ease and precision.

Scikit-learn: In the realm of machine learning, Scikit-learn is a primary tool. It provides a wide array of supervised and unsupervised learning algorithms via a consistent interface. From classification to regression, clustering, dimensionality reduction, and beyond, Scikit-learn is designed to interoperate with NumPy and Pandas for a seamless data science workflow.

TensorFlow and *Keras*: For deep learning projects, TensorFlow provides a comprehensive, flexible ecosystem of tools, libraries, and resources that enables researchers to push the state-of-the-art in ML, and developers to easily build and deploy ML-powered applications. Keras, which runs on top of TensorFlow, offers a high-level interface for neural networks, focused on enabling fast experimentation.

Beautiful Soup and *Scrapy*: For web scraping, Beautiful Soup and Scrapy are two powerful tools. Beautiful Soup is perfect for parsing HTML and XML documents, turning a webpage into a parse tree that Python can work with. Scrapy, on the other hand, is an all-encompassing web crawling and scraping framework, allowing for the extraction of data from websites automatically.

Flask and *Django*: In web development, Flask and Django are two highly-regarded frameworks. Flask is a microframework that is lightweight and easy to get started with, making it a good choice for small to medium projects and microservices. Django, more "batteries-included," handles many of the complexities of web development, such as user authentication, automatically, making it well-suited for larger, more feature-rich applications.

SQLAlchemy: For database interaction, SQLAlchemy provides a full suite of tools to effectively work with relational databases using Python. It abstracts away the complexities of SQL, allowing developers to interact with databases in a more Pythonic way. It supports a wide variety of database backends, making it versatile and powerful.

This brief overview just scratches the surface of the rich landscape of third-party Python libraries. Each library has its learning curve and best use cases, but together, they cover almost every programming need you might encounter. From performing complex data analysis, handling network requests, creating beautiful visualizations, to developing sophisticated web applications, these libraries boost productivity and open up new possibilities.

Choosing the right library for a specific task can sometimes be daunting, given the plethora of available options. However, the Python community is remarkably supportive, with vast resources like official documentation, forums, and tutorials to guide your decisions. It's always a good idea to consider the maturity of the library, its community support, and how actively it's maintained.

Adopting these third-party libraries not only enhances your Python projects but also deepens your understanding of the language and its potential applications. As you grow in your Python journey, you'll likely find yourself combining these libraries in innovative ways, further extending Python's reach. Whether you're a beginner just starting out, an intermediate programmer broadening your skills, or an advanced coder tackling complex problems, incorporating these libraries into your repertoire can propel your projects to new heights.

Ultimately, the power of Python isn't just in the language itself but also in its ecosystem. The availability and quality of these third-party libraries contribute significantly to Python's popularity and versatility, making it a preferred language across diverse fields. As you delve into these libraries and leverage their capabilities, you'll find yourself becoming not just a better Python programmer, but a more effective problem-solver, ready to tackle a wide range of challenges with confidence.

Web Frameworks: Django and Flask

The landscape of web development has evolved incredibly over the years, transitioning from simple static HTML pages to complex, dynamic applications. Python, with its simplicity and robustness, has been at the forefront of this revolution, offering two powerful frameworks for web development: Django and Flask. These frameworks provide developers with the tools necessary to build efficient, scalable, and secure web applications with ease.

Django, often referred to as "the web framework for perfectionists with deadlines," is designed to help developers build complex, database-driven websites rapidly. It follows the "batteries-included" philosophy, meaning it includes a plethora of functionalities out of the box, such as an admin panel, an ORM (Object-Relational Mapping), and authentication support. This framework is suited for projects ranging from small to large scale, making it a popular choice among startups and enterprises alike.

On the other hand, Flask is a micro-framework that prioritizes simplicity and flexibility. It provides the bare minimum to get a web application running, allowing developers to choose their tools and libraries. This "minimalist" approach makes Flask incredibly lightweight and easy to understand, especially for beginners. Flask is an excellent choice for small to medium-sized projects and for developers who prefer a "do-it-yourself" approach to web development.

When deciding between Django and Flask, it's imperative to consider the scope and requirements of your project. Django, with its extensive feature set, is ideal for developers looking to get a feature-rich application up and running without the need to seek out and integrate numerous external libraries. Its built-in features facilitate rapid development, an essential attribute for projects with tight deadlines.

Flask, being more flexible and with a shallower learning curve, is particularly well-suited for smaller projects or when you need more control over the components used in your application. Its simplicity allows developers to add only what they need, promoting a modular approach to web development. This can lead to a more tailored application architecture but may require more setup time initially.

Security is a paramount concern in web development, and both Django and Flask provide robust security features. Django comes with built-in protections against several common security threats, including SQL injection, cross-site scripting (XSS), and cross-site request forgery (CSRF). Flask also provides protection against these vulnerabilities but often relies on extensions to offer the same level of security that Django does out of the box.

One of the significant advantages of using Django is its ORM, which simplifies data manipulation and database queries. The Django ORM allows developers to interact with their database using Python code rather than SQL, speeding up the development process and reducing the risk of SQL injection attacks. Flask can also work with ORMs like SQLAlchemy, but it requires manual integration and setup.

Both Django and Flask boast large and active communities, providing ample resources for learning and troubleshooting. Django's extensive documentation, tutorials, and forums are invaluable for developers, whereas Flask's community provides a wealth of third-party extensions and detailed documentation to help customize and extend your application.

Performance is another critical factor in choosing a web framework. While both frameworks are sufficiently fast for a wide array of web applications, the "overhead" introduced by Django's additional features can make Flask a more appealing option for projects where speed is a crucial factor. However, with proper optimization, Django applications can also achieve high performance.

Deployment is a straightforward process for both Django and Flask applications, with support for various hosting platforms.

Whether you're deploying to a traditional web server or a cloud-based platform, both frameworks integrate well with services like AWS, Heroku, and Docker, simplifying the deployment process.

Flask offers more freedom in choosing the components of your application, from the ORM to the way you handle forms and authentication. This flexibility can be both a blessing and a curse, as it allows for a customized approach but also requires more decisions to be made by the developer.

Django's admin interface is one of its standout features, allowing developers and administrators to manage data easily. This auto-generated, web-based interface saves time and effort, especially during the early stages of a project when you're frequently tweaking your data models.

Both Django and Flask support developing RESTful APIs, an essential feature for modern web applications. Django Rest Framework (DRF) is a powerful and flexible toolkit for building Web APIs in Django, while Flask-RESTful provides simple tools for adding resourceful routes to your Flask application.

In conclusion, whether you're building a high-traffic social media site, a small business website, or a RESTful API, both Django and Flask offer compelling features and benefits. The choice between them depends on your project's specific needs, your familiarity with the Python ecosystem, and your personal preferences in terms of development process and application architecture. By understanding the strengths and weaknesses of each framework, you can make an informed decision that best suits your web development project.

As the world of web development continues to evolve, both Django and Flask are expected to remain popular choices among Python developers. Their strong communities, extensive documentation, and versatility make them suitable for a wide range of web development tasks, from simple websites to complex, feature-rich web applications.

Chapter 8: File Handling and I/O

Moving into the practical aspects of Python, Chapter 8 delves into the fundamental concepts of file handling and Input/Output (I/O) operations, an area that forms the backbone of many Python applications. This chapter equips readers with the knowledge to proficiently read from and write to files, a crucial skill for automating tasks, data processing, and system administration. We commence with exploring different modes of file operations, ensuring you grasp how to handle files in a way that suits your application's needs without compromising data integrity or encountering common pitfalls. Then, the chapter transitions to working with various file formats such as JSON and CSV, which are widely used in data science, web development, and configuration tasks, providing hands-on examples to parse, generate, and manipulate these formats efficiently.

Beyond text files, you'll learn about byte streams and how they differ from regular text I/O, enabling you to deal with binary files, images, or serialized data with confidence. File system management techniques are covered as well, showing you how to interact with the file system to list directories, test file existence, and more. Each concept is illustrated with code examples and best practices to ensure that you not only learn how to perform these tasks but also understand the recommended ways to approach them to write clean, efficient, and robust Python code.

Reading and Writing Files

As we delve further into Python's capabilities, a crucial skill to master is file handling. This involves reading from and writing to files, which are essential for a multitude of applications, from data analysis to automating tasks. Python provides built-in functions and methods that make these operations straightforward.

First, let's discuss reading files. Python uses the *open()* function to open a file. This function returns a file object, which has methods and attributes you can use to collect information about the file you have just opened. When reading a file, it's crucial to specify the mode. For reading, we use **'r'**. If you omit the mode argument, Python defaults to **'r'** so it's not strictly necessary but good practice to include for clarity.

Once you have a file object, you can read its content in several ways. For instance, the *read()* method reads the entire file's content into a single string. This is useful for smaller files but can be problematic with large files due to memory constraints. Alternatively, the *readline()* method reads a single line from the file each time it's called, while *readlines()* reads the entire file's contents into a list of strings.

Writing to files in Python is similarly straightforward. Instead of the **'r'** mode, you use **'w'** for writing. If the file doesn't exist, Python creates it. Be cautious, though, as opening an existing file in write mode will erase its contents. There's also the **'a'** mode for appending to the end of a file without erasing its content. The *write()* method is used to add text to the file, while *writelines()* can write a list of strings.

It's equally important to manage files properly by closing them after your operations are complete. This is where the *with* statement comes in handy, elegantly handling file opening and closing, even if exceptions occur. The syntax **with open('filename', 'r') as file:** ensures that the file is properly closed after its suite of operations is finished.

Python also offers the flexibility to work with file paths. The *os* and *os.path* modules are incredibly useful for file path manipulation, making your scripts compatible across different operating systems. They provide capabilities to join paths correctly, check for file existence, and more.

Encodings are another critical aspect of file handling. The default encoding when reading or writing files in Python is usually UTF-8, but this can be specified explicitly via the **encoding** parameter in the *open()* function. This is particularly vital when dealing with files in specific text encodings.

Error handling plays a pivotal role in file operations. Using try-except blocks around file reading/writing logic can save your script from crashing and provide valuable feedback on what went wrong. Python's built-in *IOError* and *OSError* can be caught to handle file-related errors efficiently.

For those looking to manipulate binary files, Python hasn't left you behind. Opening a file in binary mode is as simple as adding a 'b' to the mode string in the open function. This mode is crucial when dealing with non-text files, such as images or executable files.

Temporary files are often necessary for intermediate processing. Python's *tempfile* module allows for the creation of temporary files and directories. These files can be auto-deleted when they are no longer needed, helping manage disk space effectively.

File locking is occasionally needed to prevent concurrent access to a file in multi-threaded or multi-process applications. While Python's standard library doesn't provide built-in file locking mechanisms, third-party packages like *fasteners* or using system-specific solutions are available options.

As your file handling tasks become more complex, you might need to navigate file systems programmatically. The *os* module can list directory contents and traverse directory trees, allowing scripts to process files and directories in sophisticated ways.

Finally, it's worth mentioning that working with files is not just about reading and writing. It's also about understanding file system permissions, handling large files intelligently, and interacting with file metadata. Python provides the tools needed to address these aspects through its rich standard library and third-party packages.

Reading and writing files is a gateway to automation, data processing, and many other essential applications in Python. By mastering file handling, you not only enhance your Python skills but also unlock the potential for countless practical solutions to programming challenges.

Working with Different File Formats (JSON, CSV, etc.)

File handling is an essential aspect of any programming task, whether it's for data analysis, web development, or automating daily tasks. Python, with its rich set of libraries and straightforward syntax, provides powerful tools for working with different file formats, including JSON, CSV, XML, and more. In this section, we delve into handling these common file formats, highlighting the operations crucial for reading, writing, and parsing data efficiently.

Firstly, let's explore the JSON (JavaScript Object Notation) format, which is widely used for storing and exchanging data due to its lightweight nature and easy readability. Python comes with a built-in library called **json** that simplifies the process of working with JSON data. One can easily read a JSON file by using the **json.load()** method, which converts the file into a Python dictionary, allowing for easy data manipulation. Conversely, the **json.dump()** method enables you to write or append data to a JSON file, effectively serializing Python objects into JSON format.

CSV (Comma-Separated Values) files are another common file format that are often employed for storing tabular data. The Python **csv** module presents a reader and a writer object, which facilitate the reading and writing of files in CSV format. The **csv.reader()** function provides an iterator that allows for iterating over rows in the CSV file, while the **csv.writer()** object is used to create CSV files from lists or dictionaries. Furthermore, the **DictReader** and **DictWriter** classes support operations directly using dictionaries, offering a more intuitive way to work with CSV data.

While JSON and CSV are arguably the most common formats in data science and web applications, one must not overlook the relevance of XML (eXtensible Markup Language). Python's **xml.etree.ElementTree** module is a versatile tool for parsing XML files. This module treats an XML file as a tree, allowing you to navigate, search, and modify the structure and data. The approach to XML in Python is both effective and easy to comprehend, making it an invaluable asset for applications that involve configuration files, web services, and more.

In the journey of exploring these formats, it's essential to grasp the specifics of file operations. Opening a file using the **with** statement ensures that resources are efficiently managed and that files are properly closed after their operations are completed. This applies across the board, whether you're dealing with JSON, CSV, or XML files. Efficient file handling prevents data corruption and optimizes the performance of your Python scripts.

Encoding and decoding are critical considerations when working with textual data formats. The default encoding in Python 3 is UTF-8, but you may encounter files in different encodings. Being proficient in specifying the correct encoding during file operations is crucial for avoiding common pitfalls, such as character corruption or runtime errors.

Error handling is another aspect that should not be neglected. The use of try-except blocks around file operations can safeguard against unexpected failures, such as file not found errors or issues related to permissions. Moreover, validation of data, especially when reading from or writing to a file, is vital for the integrity of your application.

For those delving into data analysis or data science, understanding the handling of CSV and JSON formats can significantly enhance your data manipulation capabilities. Python's **pandas** library, for example, offers the **read_csv()** and **read_json()** functions that provide robust options for loading data into DataFrame objects, facilitating complex data analysis tasks with ease.

When it comes to web development, JSON is particularly paramount. Whether you are consuming APIs or serving data, knowing how to efficiently parse JSON data and convert Python objects to JSON format is indispensable. Frameworks like Flask and Django have built-in support for JSON, underscoring the format's ubiquity in web applications.

Automation scripts often interact with files of various formats. For instance, a script might generate a report in CSV format, pull data from a JSON API, and then modify an XML configuration file. Mastering file handling in Python enables you to write more versatile and robust automation scripts, capable of interacting with multiple data sources and services.

Security considerations must also be borne in mind, especially while dealing with file inputs and outputs. Validating and sanitizing file inputs protect your applications from malicious payloads and data corruption. Moreover, when handling file paths, use the **os.path** and **pathlib** modules to construct file paths safely, avoiding security vulnerabilities related to file path injections.

Performance optimization is a topic of interest, especially when working with large files. Techniques such as lazy loading, buffering, and leveraging libraries like **pandas** for data processing can substantially improve the efficiency of file operations in your Python applications.

In conclusion, mastering the art of file handling, particularly with diverse formats like JSON, CSV, and XML, exponentially increases the versatility of your Python programming skills. It enables you to develop applications that can effortlessly interact with various data sources, ranging from simple configuration files to complex datasets. The ability to manipulate and analyze data proficiently opens doors to opportunities in data science, web development, automation, and beyond. As you continue to hone these skills, remember that efficient and secure file handling is foundational to the success of any Python project.

Through the exploration of these topics, you are equipped to tackle file handling tasks with confidence and adaptability. This knowledge not only solidifies your foundation in Python but also prepares you for more advanced areas of application, from data science to web development. Embrace the challenges presented by different file formats, and leverage Python's ample tools and libraries to manipulate them effectively, enriching your journey through Python programming.

Byte Streams and File System Management

As we delve deeper into file handling and I/O in Python, understanding byte streams and file system management becomes imperative. Byte streams play a crucial role in reading from and writing to binary files. They are essential for dealing with binary data, such as images, videos, and executable files, where text encoding does not apply.

Python provides two main types of streams: text streams and byte streams. While text streams are decoded into strings using a specific encoding (such as UTF-8), byte streams deal with raw bytes and offer a way to handle binary data. When opening a file in binary mode by appending 'b' to the file mode in the **open()** function, Python returns a byte stream, allowing for direct manipulation of byte data.

File system management, on the other hand, involves operations such as creating, renaming, moving, or deleting files and directories. Python's **os** and **shutil** modules equip developers with a robust set of functions to navigate and manipulate the file system efficiently. Using these modules, one can automate and streamline tasks that would otherwise be tedious and error-prone.

The **os** module provides a portable way of using operating system-dependent functionality. For instance, **os.path** offers numerous utilities to work with file paths, making them adaptable across different operating systems. Functions like **os.walk()** are invaluable for recursively navigating directories, providing a systematic approach to file handling.

Python's **shutil** module complements the **os** module by offering high-level operations on files and collections of files. This includes functions to copy, move, rename, and delete files and directories. Particularly, **shutil.copy()** and **shutil.move()** abstract away the underlying file I/O operations, simplifying file management tasks.

Understanding how to manage file permissions is also critical when working with the file system. Python's **os** module allows you to modify permissions, giving you control over who can read, write, or execute a file. This control is vital in maintaining the security and integrity of the file system, especially when dealing with sensitive data.

Another aspect of file system management is dealing with symbolic links, which the **os** module also handles. Symbolic links are shortcuts to other files or directories and can be created or removed using Python's built-in functions.

Error handling is an integral part of working with byte streams and file management operations. The **try-except** block allows you to gracefully handle errors, such as **FileNotFoundError** or **PermissionError**, ensuring the robustness of your code. This is particularly important in file operations that might fail due to reasons outside your control, such as hardware issues or permission settings.

For tasks involving extensive file and directory manipulation, third-party libraries like **pathlib** offer a higher level and an object-oriented interface to the file system. Introduced in Python 3.4, **pathlib** abstracts many of the complexities of the **os** and **shutil** modules, providing a more intuitive approach to file system navigation and manipulation.

When working with large amounts of data, efficiency and optimization become paramount. Python's file handling capabilities, especially in conjunction with bytearray objects and memory views, allow for efficient manipulation and processing of large binary files. This can significantly reduce memory usage and improve the performance of your applications.

Security considerations are also crucial when dealing with file input/output operations. Sanitizing input, validating file paths, and avoiding common vulnerabilities like path injection attacks are necessary precautions. Python's built-in libraries provide tools to help secure file operations, but understanding and applying best practices in security is a responsibility that falls on developers.

In conclusion, mastering byte streams and file system management is essential for Python programmers aiming to perform comprehensive file handling operations. Whether it's reading from or writing to binary files, navigating directories, or ensuring secure and efficient file manipulation, Python offers the tools necessary to tackle these challenges. As you progress through your Python journey, integrating these concepts and techniques into your projects will not only enhance your coding skills but also open doors to new opportunities and applications.

As we move forward, the nuances of database interactions, data science applications, and web development will further demonstrate the versatility of Python in handling a wide array of programming tasks. But, understanding the foundational concepts outlined in this section will be critical in leveraging Python's full potential in these areas.

Chapter 9: Database Interaction with Python

Upon reaching Chapter 9, we delve into the potent realm of database interaction with Python, a skillset indispensable for developing applications with dynamic data management capabilities. This chapter is meticulously crafted to serve as a comprehensive guide for beginners, intermediates, and advanced Python programmers alike, aiming to equip them with the knowledge to efficiently connect, query, and manage databases using Python. We start with an introduction to SQL and SQLite, laying a solid foundation on structured query language and how to employ SQLite, a lightweight, disk-based database that doesn't require a separate server process. Following that, we explore the Object-Relational Mapping (ORM) technique with SQLAlchemy, an essential tool for Python developers that facilitates the translation of Python classes to database tables, and vice versa, using a high-level API. This abstraction allows for writing database-agnostic code, thereby enhancing code portability and maintainability.

Moving forward, the chapter transitions into the realm of NoSQL databases, highlighting their distinctions from traditional SQL databases and their suitability for handling varied data types and structures, such as JSON documents, key-value pairs, and wide-column stores. We discuss the integration of Python with popular NoSQL databases like MongoDB and Redis, providing readers with practical insights into choosing the right database for their projects and how to interact with these databases using Python. By the end of this chapter, readers will have a well-rounded understanding of database interaction with Python, equipped with the knowledge to apply these concepts to real-world applications, ranging from web development to data analytics, thus significantly expanding their Python programming horizons.

Introduction to SQL and SQLite

As we delve into the realm of database interactions with Python, understanding SQL and SQLite becomes pivotal. SQL, or Structured Query Language, is the standard language for relational database management systems. It allows users to create, read, update, and delete database records. SQLite, on the other hand, is a C-library that provides a lightweight, disk-based database. It doesn't require a separate server process, making it a perfect fit for devices with limited resources or applications that need a simple database system.

For beginners in Python, intermediate, and even advanced programmers, integrating SQL operations within Python projects can significantly enhance data manipulation and storage capabilities. SQLite, with its simplicity and efficiency, becomes the go-to option for local/client-side storage solutions. Whether the goal is to build a web application, analyze data, or create desktop tools, understanding SQLite's role in these processes is crucial.

SQLite operates by storing data in a single file, which offers a straightforward method for data management. This simplicity, however, doesn't compromise its capabilities. It supports most of the SQL standard features and is accessible on various platforms. The integration of SQLite with Python eliminates the need for external databases, simplifying the development process, especially for standalone applications or prototypes.

Python provides robust support for SQLite through the *sqlite3* module, which comes included with the standard library. This module enables Python applications to connect to an SQLite database, execute SQL queries, and manage data with minimal overhead. Its straightforward API is a testament to Python's philosophy of simplicity and inclusiveness, allowing developers to efficiently manage databases with just a few lines of code.

The process of setting up an SQLite database in Python is remarkably straightforward. With just a few lines of code, you can create a database, establish a connection, and begin executing SQL commands to manipulate data. This ease of setup is particularly appealing for small to medium-sized projects, where complex database solutions might be overkill or unnecessary.

One of the most powerful aspects of using SQLite in Python projects is the ability to direct SQL queries to interact with the database. This capability enables developers to leverage the full power of SQL within Python, blending the flexibility and versatility of both languages. Whether it's executing SELECT statements to fetch data, INSERT statements to add records, or UPDATE and DELETE statements to modify existing data, the sqlite3 module offers a comprehensive suite of tools for database operations.

Despite its simplicity, SQLite supports advanced features like transactions, which are critical for maintaining data integrity. Python's sqlite3 module allows developers to control transaction behaviors, thus providing a means to ensure that operations are atomic, consistent, isolated, and durable (ACID). By understanding transactions, developers can build more reliable and robust applications.

Data retrieval in SQLite with Python is as flexible and powerful as data manipulation. The sqlite3 module returns query results in a variety of formats, catering to different programming needs and preferences. Developers can fetch results as lists of tuples, named tuples, or dictionaries, thereby tailoring the output to the specific requirements of their applications.

Security is another important aspect of database interactions. SQLite, through its integration with Python, supports features such as parameterized queries. This not only simplifies the process of data insertion but also significantly reduces the risk of SQL injection attacks, ensuring the safety and integrity of the database.

For those looking to distribute applications, SQLite offers an attractive advantage. Since the database is entirely contained in a single file, deployment becomes a breeze. There's no need to worry about complex server configurations or database installations. The application and its database can be moved or copied just like any other file, simplifying distribution and installation.

SQLite's performance is often underestimated. While it may not match the throughput of larger database systems under heavy loads, it performs exceptionally well for small to medium-sized applications. Its efficiency and speed make it ideal for projects where simplicity and performance are key considerations.

Moreover, the open-source nature of SQLite means that it is continuously being improved and updated by a community of developers. This ensures that it remains a reliable option for Python developers. Being aware of these updates and understanding how they affect database interactions can be invaluable for maintaining modern applications.

Finally, diving into SQL and SQLite with Python opens up a world of possibilities for data management and manipulation. As we continue through this section, we'll explore practical examples and best practices for integrating SQLite in Python projects. This journey will not only enhance your coding skills but also equip you with the tools necessary for tackling real-world data challenges.

In summary, the combination of SQL's power and SQLite's simplicity with Python's versatility creates a formidable toolkit for developers. Whether you're handling data for personal projects, academic research, or professional software development, understanding how to interact with databases in Python is a critical skill that will undoubtedly enrich your programming repertoire.

ORM Usage with SQLAlchemy

Continuing from our exploration of SQL and SQLite, we delve into an advanced method of database interaction that harmonizes beautifully with Python's philosophy: using an Object-Relational Mapping (ORM) tool, specifically SQLAlchemy. ORM is a technique that connects the rich objects of an application to tables in a relational database management system. Using ORM, developers can work at a higher level of abstraction, handling databases with Pythonic classes and objects rather than raw SQL queries.

SQLAlchemy stands out as a comprehensive ORM library for Python, offering an abundance of features that facilitate the effective management of relational databases. It abstracts away the complexities of SQL, allowing developers to focus on the interactive Python code instead. By marrying the relational database systems with Object-Oriented Programming concepts, SQLAlchemy not only optimizes database operations but also enhances code readability and maintainability.

To start using SQLAlchemy, one must first install it, typically via pip. After installation, the core of SQLAlchemy's ORM usage begins with the definition of models. Models in SQLAlchemy are Python classes that inherit from `Base`, a declarative base that maintains a catalog of classes and tables relating to those classes.

Defining a model involves declaring a class that defines the table structure in its attributes, where each attribute represents a column in the database table. SQLAlchemy leverages Python's decorators and

Field Types to map these class properties to database columns seamlessly.

After models are defined, the next step involves creating an engine and a session. The engine is fundamental in SQLAlchemy as it establishes the connection with the database. Through the session, developers can query the database using the ORM, which translates high-level operations into SQL queries.

The session facilitates a pattern known as Unit of Work, which maintains a coherence between the objects in your application and the rows in the database. This pattern ensures that all changes made to objects are either committed or rolled back simultaneously, thus maintaining database integrity.

Querying in SQLAlchemy is remarkably intuitive. Instead of writing raw SQL, developers can use the rich API provided by SQLAlchemy to execute queries. This involves calling methods on the session object or the model classes, which SQLAlchemy translates into SQL queries automatically. The result of these queries is returned as instances of the model class, enabling a seamless integration between the database records and the Python objects.

Transactions in SQLAlchemy are handled through the session. Any operation that modifies the database is not finalized until `session.commit()` is called. This mechanism provides a means to roll back changes in case of an error, thus safeguarding the database's integrity.

SQLAlchemy also supports relationships between tables, including one-to-many and many-to-many relationships. Defining these relationships in SQLAlchemy is straightforward, involving the use of relationship fields in models. These relationships once defined, allow for the use of joined queries, which SQLAlchemy can optimize for performance.

One of the strengths of SQLAlchemy is its ability to work across multiple database systems. Regardless of whether you're using SQLite, PostgreSQL, MySQL, or another SQL dialect, SQLAlchemy provides a consistent API for all. This universality ensures that your application is portable and adaptable to various database systems with minimal changes to the ORM layer.

Performance in SQLAlchemy is a common concern, especially for those transitioning from raw SQL. It's important to note that while there is overhead associated with abstracting SQL into ORM operations, SQLAlchemy offers numerous optimization features. These include lazy loading, eager loading, and the ability to drop down into raw SQL when necessary. Understanding these features and using them appropriately can mitigate performance concerns.

Migrating an existing database to use with SQLAlchemy is also achievable through tools like Alembic, which is specifically designed for database migrations. Alembic allows the incremental, version-controlled modification of database schemas, making it possible to adapt an existing database to an ORM model with relative ease.

In conclusion, ORM usage with SQLAlchemy provides a powerful, efficient, and Pythonic way of interacting with relational databases. By understanding and leveraging the features and best practices of SQLAlchemy, developers can significantly streamline database operations in their applications, leading to cleaner, more maintainable code. As with any advanced tool, the key to getting the most out of SQLAlchemy lies in investing time in learning its intricacies and subtleties.

The journey from SQL queries to ORM with SQLAlchemy represents a significant leap in abstraction, enabling developers to operate at a higher level of thought when interacting with databases. This transition is not only a testament to the flexibility and power of Python as a programming language but also to the vibrant ecosystem of libraries and frameworks that support its usage across a wide array of applications.

NoSQL Databases & Python

Transitioning from the structured world of SQL, it's crucial for Python developers to acquaint themselves with the realm of NoSQL databases. NoSQL, or "Not Only SQL," encompasses a broad array of database technologies designed to address the limitations of traditional relational databases. Given Python's versatility and its widespread use in data-centric applications, understanding how to interact with NoSQL databases is an indispensable skill for developers.

At the core of NoSQL databases is their ability to store and manage unstructured data. They offer flexibility, scalability, and high performance in handling vast volumes of data, making them an ideal choice for big data and real-time web applications. Popular NoSQL databases such as MongoDB, Cassandra, Redis, and Couchbase have distinct characteristics, but they all share the commonality of being schema-less, which contrasts sharply with the rigid, table-based structure of SQL databases.

Python, with its simplicity and rich ecosystem, provides robust support for interacting with NoSQL databases. Libraries and drivers for various NoSQL databases are readily available, enabling Python developers to seamlessly connect to, query, and manipulate data. For instance, the **pymongo** library facilitates interaction with MongoDB, while the **redis-py** library allows for easy manipulation of Redis databases.

Getting started with NoSQL in Python typically involves installing the appropriate library or driver for the chosen database. Using the MongoDB example, one would start by installing **pymongo** using pip, Python's package installer. The process is straightforward and similar across various NoSQL databases, highlighting Python's ease of use and its compatibility with NoSQL technology.

Once set up, connecting to a NoSQL database from Python is generally a matter of a few lines of code. Developers specify connection parameters such as the database address and port, and then they can commence executing queries. The syntax and functions used may vary depending on the database and library, but the simplicity and readability of Python remain constant.

Querying a NoSQL database from Python can differ significantly from SQL due to the lack of a universal query language. MongoDB, for example, uses a document-oriented model, and queries are represented as JSON-like structures. Learning to think in the database's query language while coding in Python is a skill that develops over time but is facilitated by Python's natural data handling capabilities.

Inserting, updating, and deleting data in NoSQL databases through Python also follows the pattern of simplicity. The operations closely align with their counterparts in traditional databases but are tailored to the document, key-value, or other data models specific to NoSQL systems. Python's data structures, such as dictionaries and lists, integrate well with the data models of NoSQL databases, simplifying data manipulation.

Handling complex data types and large datasets is where NoSQL databases truly shine in combination with Python. The flexibility in schema and data modeling allows for the storage of nested and heterogeneous data sets that are commonplace in applications such as content management systems, e-commerce platforms, and scientific data analysis.

Scaling applications with NoSQL and Python is another area that highlights the strengths of both. NoSQL databases are designed to scale out horizontally, and Python's simplicity allows developers to focus on optimizing application logic rather than worrying about the intricacies of the database layer.

Of course, integrating NoSQL databases with Python is not without its challenges. The lack of a fixed schema, while offering flexibility, can lead to data inconsistency if not managed properly. Furthermore, the diversity among NoSQL databases means developers must adapt to different data models, querying languages, and consistency models.

Security is another critical aspect when working with NoSQL databases and Python. Ensuring data is securely stored and accessed requires developers to implement proper authentication, encryption, and access control mechanisms. Python libraries for NoSQL databases often include features for securing database connections and data, but it demands due diligence from developers to utilize these features correctly.

Efficiently integrating NoSQL databases into Python applications often entails leveraging additional tools and libraries. For instance, ORMs (Object-Relational Mappings) are not as common or necessary in NoSQL, but ODMs (Object-Document Mappings) for document databases like MongoDB can simplify data interaction further.

Furthermore, the dynamic and evolving ecosystem of NoSQL databases means that Python developers must stay informed about the latest advancements and best practices. Participating in community discussions, exploring new libraries, and continuously experimenting with different databases are effective ways to enhance one's skills and knowledge in this area.

In conclusion, the interaction of NoSQL databases with Python embodies the dynamic, flexible, and powerful capabilities necessary for modern application development. Embracing the principles of

NoSQL and learning to effectively utilize these databases within Python applications opens up new possibilities for innovation, scalability, and performance. As with any technology, mastering NoSQL databases in the context of Python programming is an iterative learning process, but it's one that can lead to highly rewarding outcomes.

Chapter 10: Python for Data Science and Analysis

In this chapter, we dive deep into the utilization of Python in the fields of data science and analysis, harnessing the power of its libraries and tools that are specifically tailored for these tasks. Python has emerged as a go-to language for data scientists and analysts worldwide not only due to its ease of use but also because of its rich ecosystem of libraries that simplify complex data operations. Among the most crucial tools in a data scientist's arsenal are NumPy and Pandas, which provide an extensive range of functionalities for numerical computation and data manipulation, respectively. While NumPy offers powerful array objects and functions to perform mathematical operations over large datasets efficiently, Pandas is praised for its DataFrame objects that enable clear and concise handling, manipulation, and analysis of structured data.

Data visualization is another critical aspect covered in this chapter, with libraries such as Matplotlib and Seaborn making it possible to convert data into highly insightful graphical representations. Through these tools, readers will learn how to generate a variety of plots, charts, and graphs that illustrate the patterns, correlations, and trends hidden within data. By the end of this chapter, readers, whether beginners or those with intermediate or advanced Python skills, seeking to apply Python in data science and analysis will have a solid understanding of how to wield these powerful libraries to extract valuable insights from data and present their findings in a visually compelling manner.

NumPy for Numerical Computation

Continuing our journey into the rich and varied landscape of Python for data science and analysis, we enter the realm of numerical computation. At the heart of this domain lies the NumPy library, a cornerstone for any data scientist or analyst working in Python. NumPy, which stands for Numerical Python, provides an efficient interface to store and operate on dense data buffers. Understanding NumPy is imperative for anyone looking to delve into data analysis, machine learning, or scientific computing with Python.

NumPy arrays, the central feature of the library, differ significantly from Python's built-in list data type. These arrays are more compact, faster, and provide a wider array of operations that are crucial for numerical computations. The fundamental advantage of NumPy arrays lies in their ability to perform vectorized operations, which means operations on entire arrays can be carried out without the need for loops. This not only simplifies the code but also dramatically increases the performance.

One of the first concepts to grasp when working with NumPy is the concept of broadcasting. Broadcasting is a powerful mechanism that allows NumPy to work with arrays of different shapes when performing arithmetic operations. Essentially, it enables automatic expansion of dimensions of the smaller array to match the larger one, thereby simplifying operations between arrays of different sizes.

Another important aspect of NumPy is its ability to perform indexing and slicing on arrays. NumPy provides more flexible indexing than regular Python lists, including indexing with arrays of indices, boolean indexing, and more. This allows for very efficient selection and manipulation of data within arrays.

The mathematical functions available in NumPy are expansive. From basic arithmetic operations to complex trigonometric, statistical, and algebraic functions, NumPy serves as a comprehensive toolkit for numerical computation. These functions are highly optimized for performance and are designed to work effectively with NumPy arrays.

NumPy also integrates seamlessly with a wide variety of databases, making it an invaluable tool for data science and analysis. It can handle data in various formats and is capable of interfacing with data from text files, images, sound clips, and binary files. This versatility is essential for data scientists who often work with diverse datasets.

The efficiency of NumPy stems from its implementation in C and Fortran. This ensures that operations on NumPy arrays, even for large amounts of data, are executed swiftly. This efficiency is vital in data science, where processing large datasets is commonplace. The ability to perform high-speed computations on numerical data is a significant advantage of using NumPy.

For those looking to delve deeper into scientific computing, NumPy serves as the foundation upon which many other scientific computing libraries are built. Libraries such as SciPy, Matplotlib, and Pandas are built on top of NumPy, leveraging its array operations and computational efficiency. This ecosystem of libraries creates a powerful toolset for data analysis and visualization.

An understanding of NumPy array manipulation is crucial for effective data preprocessing in machine learning. Many machine learning algorithms expect data to be structured in specific ways, often as NumPy arrays. Being adept at reshaping, transforming, and preparing data with NumPy ensures a smooth transition to advanced analytics and machine learning model building.

Memory management in NumPy is another area where its capabilities shine. NumPy arrays have a fixed size at creation, unlike Python lists which can grow dynamically. This design choice allows for more efficient allocation of memory and ensures that memory consumption is predictable and manageable, an essential aspect when working with large datasets.

NumPy not only excels in handling numerical data but also supports an array of numerical datatypes more extensive than those available in Python. This support includes complex numbers, fixed-precision integers, and floating-point numbers with customizable precision. Such granularity in numerical precision is incredibly beneficial for scientific calculations and financial analyses where accuracy is paramount.

The community and ecosystem around NumPy are substantial. With comprehensive documentation, a plethora of tutorials, and an active community forum, getting started or solving complex problems becomes much easier. The wealth of resources available ensures that learners and professionals alike can effectively harness the capabilities of NumPy.

In summary, NumPy stands as a pillar of the Python data science ecosystem. Its versatile array objects, broad suite of mathematical functions, and compatibility with a wide array of data formats make it an indispensable tool for anyone engaging in numerical computation, data analysis, or scientific research in Python. For beginners, familiarizing yourselves with NumPy arrays and operations opens the door to advanced data manipulations and analyses. For the intermediate and seasoned programmers, NumPy's efficiency and integrations serve as a means to tackle complex, data-intensive challenges.

As we progress further into topics such as data manipulation with Pandas and data visualization tools, the foundational knowledge of NumPy will serve to enhance the understanding and application of these subsequent tools and libraries. Thus, mastering NumPy is not just about learning a library; it's about equipping oneself with the computational tools to explore, analyze, and interpret the world of data.

Data Manipulation with Pandas

Within the spectrum of Python libraries, Pandas stands out for data analysis and manipulation. Originating as an open-source project, its purpose is to offer powerful, expressive, and flexible data structures designed to make working with "relational" or "labeled" data both intuitive and easy. As we delve further, we shall explore the fundamentals and advanced functionalities of Pandas, guiding beginners through its capabilities, and offering insights that intermediate and advanced Python programmers will find beneficial.

Pandas primarily provides two data structures, Series and DataFrame, which allow for efficient manipulation of one-dimensional and two-dimensional data respectively. The Series represents a one-dimensional labeled array capable of holding any data type, while the DataFrame is somewhat akin to a relational data table, with rows and columns of potentially different types. Understanding these structures is pivotal for effective data manipulation.

Starting with data importing, Pandas supports a plethora of formats, ranging from CSV, Excel, SQL databases, and JSON, to name a few. This capability ensures that data analysts can easily import data from diverse sources, transforming raw data into actionable insights with minimal preprocessing. Through simple commands, Pandas allows for straightforward reading and writing of files, making it an invaluable tool for those dealing with varied data sources.

Data cleaning is another area where Pandas excels. The library comes equipped with a variety of functions designed to handle missing values, duplicate data, and unwanted characters. Such pre-processing tasks, though seemingly mundane, are crucial steps in data analysis. By streamlining these processes, Pandas allows analysts to focus more on extracting insights rather than getting bogged down by data munging issues.

Moreover, Pandas offers extensive capabilities for data exploration and analysis. Functions like **describe()**, **mean()**, **median()**, and **mode()** provide quick statistical summaries of the datasets. These are complemented by powerful grouping and pivoting functionalities that allow for sophisticated data aggregation and cross-tabulation, enabling users to perform complex analyses with relative ease.

One of Pandas' most significant features is its handling of time series data. Time series manipulation is inherently complex due to its sequential nature and often requires specialized functionality for resampling, time shifts, and window functions. Pandas was designed with strong support for temporal data manipulations, making it an indispensable tool for financial, economic, and environmental data analysis, where time series data is prevalent.

Pandas integrates seamlessly with other scientific and analytical Python libraries. For instance, its close relationship with NumPy allows for high-performance operations on large datasets, while its compatibility with libraries like Matplotlib and Seaborn facilitates sophisticated data visualizations directly from DataFrame objects. This interoperability not only enriches the Python ecosystem for data science but also streamlines workflows, allowing for more cohesive analyses.

On the topic of performance, while Pandas is primarily backed by Python, critical parts of its library are written in Cython to achieve speed improvements where necessary. Performance-wise, it's optimized for both small and large data sets, making it suitable for a wide range of data science tasks, from quick analyses on modest datasets to large-scale data processing on multi-gigabyte datasets.

Data transformation is a forte of Pandas, thanks to its comprehensive set of features for filtering, sorting, and altering datasets. These transformations are essential for preparing data for analysis or machine learning models. Whether it's merging different datasets, pivoting tables, or applying custom functions to data, Pandas provides a fluent and intuitive syntax, making these operations both straightforward and efficient.

Conditional operations play a crucial role in data analysis. Pandas adeptly handles these through Boolean indexing, allowing users to filter data based on complex criteria easily. This feature greatly enhances the library's utility by facilitating the extraction of relevant information from massive datasets, a common requirement in data-driven decision-making processes.

While Pandas is a powerhouse for data manipulation, it's crucial to note that it is also designed with extensibility in mind. It can interact with a vast ecosystem of data sources, analysis tools, and visualization libraries. This aspect is particularly important in the dynamically evolving field of data science, where the ability to adapt and integrate with other tools can significantly amplify a data scientist's productivity and impact.

Error handling in Pandas is executed with a clear and informative approach. The library provides detailed error messages and warnings, guiding users to quickly identify and rectify issues in their code. This feature is particularly beneficial for beginners, as it aids in understanding and debugging the intricate process of data manipulation.

Lastly, the vibrant community and comprehensive documentation surrounding Pandas play a pivotal role in its adoption and use. Newcomers and experienced users alike will find a plethora of tutorials, forums, and discussion groups dedicated to Pandas, which offer valuable resources for learning and troubleshooting. The community's contribution to continual improvement and enhancement of the library ensures that it stays relevant and robust for various applications.

In conclusion, Pandas is a linchpin library in the Python ecosystem for data science and analysis. Its blend of power, flexibility, and ease of use makes it a vital tool for anyone tasked with data manipulation tasks. Whether you're cleaning data, performing complex transformations, or analyzing time series, Pandas provides the means to do so effectively and efficiently. With its impressive capabilities and strong community support, learning Pandas is a worthwhile investment for anyone looking to deepen their data analysis skills.

As we progress through this chapter, we'll delve deeper into practical examples and advanced features, equipping you with the knowledge to harness the full potential of Pandas in your data science endeavors. Thus, understanding and mastering Pandas not only contributes to individual skill development but also empowers Python programmers to tackle a broad array of challenges in data analysis and beyond.

Data Visualization Tools (Matplotlib, Seaborn)

When diving into the world of Python for Data Science and Analysis, a pivotal moment arises when we discuss the visualization of data. Two tools stand out in the Python ecosystem for their robustness, versatility, and ease of use: Matplotlib and Seaborn. These libraries serve as a bridge between the raw, complex data and actionable insights by creating interpretable and visually engaging representations of the data.

Matplotlib, a foundation stone in Python visualization libraries, offers extensive options for creating static, animated, and interactive visualizations. It's an indispensable tool for data scientists who need a high degree of customization in their plots and those who are working on academic articles or presentations that require precise formatting. Its design is highly adaptable, allowing users to tweak nearly every element of a plot from titles and labels to axes limits and styles.

However, the real power of Matplotlib shines when you start to understand its hierarchy of objects. At the top level is the Matplotlib figure, a container that holds all parts of a plot. Within a figure are one or more axes, each containing elements that make up the plot, including line styles, legend labels, tick labels, and text boxes. This hierarchical structure may seem daunting at first, but it allows for detailed control over every plot element.

On the other hand, Seaborn operates on a higher level of abstraction. Built on top of Matplotlib, it provides a more straightforward interface for creating beautifully styled statistical plots. Seaborn comes with a variety of built-in themes and color palettes, making it easy to create aesthetically pleasing visualizations with minimal code. It's particularly adept at handling complex dataset structures natively, enabling comprehensive visual data exploration with simpler syntax.

One of Seaborn's strengths is its ability to summarize and present data insights through complex visualizations like heatmaps, violin plots, and pair plots, with less syntactical requirements than Matplotlib. These visualizations are not only visually striking but are also packed with data insights, making them favored in exploratory data analysis.

It's also important to note the complementarity between Matplotlib and Seaborn. While Seaborn leverages Matplotlib for its foundational plotting capabilities, users can drop down to Matplotlib for fine-tuning. This synergy allows for the creation of sophisticated visualizations that benefit from both Seaborn's simplicity and Matplotlib's flexibility.

For beginners, starting with Matplotlib's basic plots can be an excellent way to understand the fundamentals of data visualization. Gradually, as one becomes more comfortable, introducing Seaborn to take advantage of its data-aware paradigms can significantly streamline the visualization process. Many tutorials and resources are available to guide this learning curve, helping users to quickly move from generating simple line charts to complex multidimensional plots.

The practical applications of these tools in data science are vast. Visual data exploration with Seaborn can uncover hidden patterns and relationships that might not be evident from looking at raw data alone. Similarly, the precision offered by Matplotlib is invaluable for preparing publication-quality figures. Whether it's for internal data analysis, academic research, or client presentations, mastering these tools can greatly enhance the presentation and interpretation of data.

Furthermore, the active development and widespread use of both libraries ensure they stay relevant and powerful. Their open-source nature has fostered a vibrant community of contributors who continuously add new features and improvements. This means that as Python and its ecosystem evolve, Matplotlib and Seaborn will continue to offer cutting-edge visualization capabilities.

However, proficiency in these tools goes beyond merely knowing the syntax. Effective data visualization requires an understanding of best practices in visual communication. This includes selecting the right type of plot for the data, using color and shape effectively to convey information, and creating readable and informative charts that tell a story about the data.

While learning to use Matplotlib and Seaborn, it's beneficial to experiment with real datasets. Hands-on practice helps in understanding how different types of data behave and how best to represent them visually. Through iterative experimentation, one can hone their ability to create insightful and impactful visualizations.

In conclusion, Matplotlib and Seaborn are indispensable tools in the Python data science toolkit. Their combination of power, flexibility, and ease of use makes them ideal for a wide range of data visualization tasks. As you advance in your Python journey, continually refining your visualization skills with these tools will prove invaluable in transforming data into compelling stories and actionable insights.

As we proceed to the next sections, we'll delve deeper into how these libraries can be integrated into more complex data science workflows, exploring their roles in machine learning, web applications, and beyond. The journey from data to insights is a critical path in modern data science, and Matplotlib and Seaborn are key companions on this journey. Let's embrace these tools with enthusiasm and creativity to unlock the full potential of our data.

Chapter 11: Python for Machine Learning

Transitioning smoothly from the theoretical underpinnings covered in our Data Science and Analysis discussions, this chapter ventures into the captivating world of Machine Learning (ML) with Python at its core. The ascent of ML has been nothing short of revolutionary in the tech realm, offering unprecedented insights and automation across diverse sectors. Python's simplicity, coupled with its powerful libraries, makes it an ideal candidate for both newcomers and seasoned professionals looking to dive into ML. We begin with a solid introduction to fundamental ML concepts, ensuring a strong foundation before moving on to more intricate subjects. Recognizing the pivotal role of libraries in this ecosystem, we put a spotlight on Scikit-Learn, an indispensable tool for ML in Python due to its robust, easy-to-use machine learning algorithms. The exploration deepens as we delve into the realms of TensorFlow and Keras, where the potential of deep learning—a subset of machine learning known for its prowess in handling vast arrays of data—is unlocked. This section aims not just to enlighten but also to empower readers with the capability to implement practical machine learning models. Through a blend of theoretical knowledge and hands-on exercises, the chapter is meticulously crafted to offer a comprehensive understanding of machine learning's paradigms, challenges, and, more importantly, its implementation using Python's ecosystem.

Introduction to Machine Learning Concepts

As the journey in understanding Python's vast applications continues, the focus shifts to a transformative and rapidly evolving domain: machine learning (ML). The essence of machine learning, a subset of artificial intelligence, lies in its ability to empower programs to autonomously learn and adapt from data without being explicitly programmed for every conceivable scenario. This introduction aims to demystify the core concepts of machine learning, setting a solid foundation for subsequent exploration and practical application using Python.

At its heart, machine learning involves algorithms that parse data, learn from that data, and then apply what they've learned to make informed decisions. Imagine a program that can predict the price of a stock, the outcome of a game, or even a patient's diagnosis based on symptoms. Such prowess doesn't come from hand-coded logic for each possibility but from learning patterns within the data it is fed.

Machine learning's real-world applications are diverse and impactful. From email filtering that distinguishes between spam and important messages to recommendation systems that suggest products, movies, or songs based on user behavior, ML algorithms enhance our daily lives in ways both overt and subtle. In the realms of healthcare, finance, and beyond, these algorithms offer the promise of increased efficiency, deeper insights, and in some cases, breakthrough innovations.

The allure of machine learning lies not only in its applications but also in the variety of techniques and theories it encompasses. Supervised learning, where algorithms learn from labeled training data to predict outcomes or classify data into groups, offers a direct approach to predictive analytics. Unsupervised learning, by contrast, deals with finding hidden patterns or intrinsic structures in input data without labeled responses. Reinforcement learning, a paradigm where algorithms learn to make decisions through trial and error, represents a closer step towards human-like artificial intelligence by seeking to mimic the way humans learn from interacting with their environment.

For those embarking on their machine learning journey, Python stands out as a language of choice due to its simplicity, readability, and robust ecosystem. Libraries and frameworks like Scikit-Learn, TensorFlow, and Keras have democratized access to machine learning, providing tools that abstract the complex mathematics and algorithms underlying ML models. These tools enable both novice and experienced programmers to build, experiment with, and deploy machine learning applications.

Understanding data is the first step in machine learning. Data preprocessing, a critical phase, involves cleaning and converting raw data into a format that algorithms can effectively process. This might include handling missing values, normalizing data to a specific range, and encoding categorical variables into numerical format. Such meticulous preparation ensures that the data feeding into a model is conducive to learning.

Feature selection and engineering further refine the dataset. By selecting the most relevant features or creating new features from existing ones, one can significantly influence the performance of a machine learning model. This process requires a blend of domain expertise and analytical skills to identify which data attributes most strongly predict the desired outcome.

The choice of algorithm depends on the problem at hand, the nature of the data, and the desired output. While some algorithms like decision trees and linear regression are more interpretable, others, like neural networks, offer higher complexity and predictive power at the expense of transparency. Balancing the trade-off between accuracy and interpretability is a common theme in the development of machine learning solutions.

Model evaluation is another cornerstone of machine learning. Techniques like cross-validation and performance metrics such as accuracy, precision, recall, and F1 score provide insights into a model's effectiveness. These evaluation methods help in fine-tuning models and selecting the approach that best fits the problem's specific constraints and objectives.

However, machine learning is not without its challenges. Issues such as overfitting, where a model learns the training data too well but performs poorly on unseen data, and underfitting, where a model is too simple to capture the underlying pattern of the data, recur frequently. Striking the right balance requires skill, experience, and sometimes, a bit of intuition.

Ethical considerations also play a significant role in machine learning. As algorithms increasingly influence aspects of daily life, concerns about bias, fairness, and accountability come to the forefront. Ensuring that models do not perpetuate or amplify biases present in the training data is both a technical challenge and a moral imperative.

Despite these challenges, the future of machine learning is incredibly promising. Advances in computational power, algorithms, and data availability continue to push the boundaries of what's possible. From autonomous vehicles to personalized medicine, the potential applications of machine learning are vast and varied.

For those poised to dive into machine learning with Python, the path is replete with opportunities for innovation and discovery. Through persistence, creativity, and the continuous acquisition of knowledge, enthusiasts can leverage machine learning to solve complex problems, gain actionable insights, and contribute to the advancement of this dynamic field.

In conclusion, machine learning offers a captivating blend of theoretical challenges and practical applications. Its concepts are at the forefront of discussions about the future of technology and its role in society. By integrating these concepts with Python, one of the most popular programming languages, learners and practitioners equip themselves with the tools to not only participate in these discussions but to shape the future themselves.

Thus, this introduction sets the stage for a deeper dive into machine learning with Python, encouraging a hands-on approach to learning and experimentation. As we move forward, the subsequent sections will cover the practical aspects of implementing these concepts, leveraging Python's rich ecosystem to build and deploy machine learning models effectively.

Scikit-Learn for Machine Learning

Embarking on the machine learning journey with Python, it's essential to become acquainted with scikit-learn, one of the most popular and efficient libraries for machine learning tasks. Scikit-learn offers a wide array of algorithms for both supervised and unsupervised learning, wrapped in a user-friendly interface that integrates seamlessly with the broader Python scientific ecosystem, including libraries such as NumPy and pandas.

Beyond the simplicity of its API, scikit-learn provides detailed documentation and tutorials that serve as indispensable resources for learners at all levels. These materials don't just cover the "how" of executing machine learning tasks but also delve into the "why," providing insights into algorithm selection and the nuances of model tuning.

At its core, scikit-learn emphasizes consistency and reusability, making it easier to experiment with different models. For example, a user can switch from using a simple linear regression model to a complex ensemble method with minimal changes to their code. This simplicity in transitioning between models fosters a learning environment that encourages experimentation and hands-on learning.

One foundational aspect of machine learning that scikit-learn helps demystify is the concept of training and testing datasets. The library provides functions to split data easily, allowing for the evaluation of model performance and the prevention of issues like overfitting. Through practical exercises, users can grasp the importance of these concepts in building reliable and robust machine learning models.

Furthermore, feature extraction and processing are pivotal in machine learning pipelines, and scikit-learn offers a comprehensive set of tools for these tasks. From handling categorical variables to standardizing numerical features, the library ensures data is optimally formatted before it's fed into a learning algorithm. This aspect of scikit-learn is crucial for beginners to understand, as proper data preprocessing can significantly impact model performance.

Another significant advantage of scikit-learn is its approach to model evaluation. The library provides a wealth of metrics and scoring methods suited to various machine learning tasks, be it regression, classification, or clustering. Learning to evaluate models accurately is an essential skill in machine learning, enabling practitioners to iteratively improve their models based on quantitative feedback.

Hyperparameter tuning is another area where scikit-learn excels. Through utilities like GridSearchCV and RandomizedSearchCV, users can methodically explore combinations of parameters to find the most effective model settings. This process, while computationally intensive, is made accessible through scikit-learn's intuitive interface, allowing users to gain hands-on experience with one of the more nuanced aspects of machine learning.

For those engaged in unsupervised learning, scikit-learn provides a variety of clustering algorithms and techniques for dimensionality reduction. These tools are invaluable for tasks such as customer segmentation or feature discovery, serving as a gateway for beginners to explore machine learning applications beyond predictive modeling.

Scikit-learn also places a strong emphasis on collaboration and community contribution, embodying the spirit of open-source development. The library is continually improved and updated, with contributions from a diverse user base that ranges from academia to industry. This community-driven development ensures that scikit-learn remains at the cutting edge of machine learning technologies.

While scikit-learn offers extensive functionality, it's designed to work well with other libraries, particularly for tasks such as deep learning, where TensorFlow and Keras might be more suitable. However, for those starting in machine learning, scikit-learn provides a comprehensive, approachable foundation, enabling learners to build a solid understanding of basic concepts before delving into more specialized libraries and tools.

In practice, mastering scikit-learn involves working on real-world datasets and problems. Whether it's predicting housing prices, classifying hand-written digits, or segmenting client bases, the library offers the tools necessary to tackle a broad range of machine learning projects. Learners are encouraged to apply the concepts and techniques learned to their datasets, facilitating a deeper understanding through practical application.

As this section progresses, the focus will turn to more specific examples and tutorials that highlight scikit-learn's capabilities. Starting with basic tasks and gradually moving to more complex machine learning challenges, these hands-on exercises will help consolidate understanding and build confidence in applying scikit-learn to solve real-world problems.

Finally, while scikit-learn is a powerful tool for machine learning, it's important to recognize that mastering it is only part of the journey. Continuous learning and adaptation to new methods and technologies are crucial in the fast-evolving field of machine learning. Still, the solid foundation provided by scikit-learn will undoubtedly serve learners well, as they progress in their machine learning endeavours.

In conclusion, scikit-learn stands as an integral part of the Python ecosystem for machine learning. It offers an accessible yet powerful gateway for those seeking to apply machine learning concepts, bridging the gap between theoretical understanding and practical application. Through scikit-learn, beginners and seasoned practitioners alike can explore the fascinating world of machine learning, armed with the tools necessary for success.

Deep Learning with TensorFlow and Keras

The advent of deep learning has marked a significant milestone in our ability to understand complex data patterns and make predictions with unprecedented accuracy. As we delve into this chapter on deep learning with TensorFlow and Keras, it's imperative to understand that these tools offer a formidable array for developing and training machine learning models. TensorFlow, developed by Google, and Keras, now integrated with TensorFlow as its official high-level API, together form a powerful duo that simplifies the process of building and deploying machine learning models.

Starting with TensorFlow, it's a versatile library for numerical computation that enables machine learning practitioners to construct and train complex models with ease. TensorFlow's architecture allows for deployment across a variety of platforms, from desktops to cluster servers, and even on mobile devices, making it a universally applicable tool in the field of machine learning. Its computation graph abstraction provides a clear-cut structure for defining data flow and operations, hence facilitating a more intuitive development process.

On the other hand, Keras functions as an interface for TensorFlow, focusing on being user-friendly, modular, and extensible. It is designed for humans, not machines, emphasizing an easy approach to deep learning. Keras serves as the ideal starting point for beginners venturing into the world of deep learning due to its simple syntax. However, do not mistake its simplicity for lack of power. Keras is capable of building sophisticated models that can compete with the best in terms of accuracy and efficiency.

The combination of TensorFlow's comprehensive tools and Keras's high-level APIs has democratized deep learning, making it accessible to not only seasoned data scientists but also to beginners and enthusiasts embarking on their Python and machine learning journey. This synergy allows for the swift implementation of neural networks, with less focus on the intricate boilerplate code often associated with lower-level programming interfaces.

Before diving into deep learning models, it's crucial to grasp the fundamentals of neural networks, the backbone of deep learning. Neural networks are inspired by the biological neural networks in human brains, albeit simplified for computational efficiency. Understanding the structure of neural networks, including layers, neurons, weights, and activation functions, is essential for anyone looking to explore deep learning.

TensorFlow and Keras facilitate the construction of these neural networks through layers abstraction, which can be stacked to build complex deep learning models. TensorFlow 2.x has embraced Keras as its official high-level API, which means that using Keras is now the recommended way to create and train neural networks with TensorFlow as the backend.

A significant advantage of using TensorFlow and Keras for deep learning is their vast ecosystem, encompassing tools and libraries for data loading, augmentation, and preprocessing. This ecosystem includes TensorBoard, which offers visualization of training processes, and TensorFlow Datasets, which provides a plethora of datasets ready to be used for training. Access to pre-trained models, through TensorFlow Hub, is also a game-changer, allowing practitioners to leverage existing models for transfer learning, reducing both the time and data needed for training new models.

Getting started with TensorFlow and Keras involves setting up the Python environment with the necessary libraries. For those who aim to utilize GPUs for training acceleration, additional steps to configure TensorFlow to use the GPU are required. However, TensorFlow provides comprehensive documentation and community support, making this process as smooth as possible.

One of the first practical steps in learning TensorFlow and Keras is understanding model architecture. Keras simplifies model construction through its Sequential API, which is ideal for beginners, as it allows for the linear stacking of layers to build neural networks. More complex architectures can be achieved using the Functional API, offering the flexibility needed for creating models with shared layers, multiple inputs, and outputs.

Training a deep learning model with TensorFlow and Keras involves compiling the model with an optimizer, loss function, and metrics for performance evaluation. Keras simplifies this process, allowing beginners to focus more on model architecture and less on the boilerplate code associated with these steps. The training process itself is executed using the **.fit()** method, where data is fed to the model, and the backpropagation algorithm adjusts the model's weights to minimize the loss.

After training, evaluating the model's performance is critical. TensorFlow and Keras provide methods for assessing accuracy and other metrics on a test set, giving insight into how well the model generalizes to unseen data. Fine-tuning and adjusting the model based on these evaluations can significantly improve performance.

Moreover, once a model has been satisfactorily trained and tested, it can be deployed for inference, predicting outcomes based on new data. TensorFlow and Keras support the saving and loading of models, allowing them to be used in production environments, mobile applications, and web services.

Deep learning with TensorFlow and Keras offers an exciting and dynamic field full of possibilities. Whether you're processing image data, analyzing sequences for natural language processing, or exploring generative models, TensorFlow and Keras provide the tools and flexibility needed to bring cutting-edge models to life. This blend of power and simplicity makes deep learning more approachable than ever, empowering professionals and enthusiasts alike to push the boundaries of what's possible with machine learning.

In conclusion, TensorFlow and Keras stand at the forefront of deep learning, offering a balance between accessibility and functionality. As we continue to explore these tools, the potential applications of deep learning expand, ushering in a new era of innovation that will undoubtedly transform industries and societies. The journey from understanding the basics of neural networks to deploying sophisticated models has never been more facilitated, making now an opportune time to embark on your deep learning adventure with Python.

Chapter 12: Automating Tasks with Python Scripts

In the journey of harnessing Python's extensive capabilities, automating routine or complex tasks stands out as an immensely valuable skill set for individuals across various proficiency levels, from beginners to seasoned developers. Python, with its straightforward syntax and powerful standard library, enables the automation of daily tasks efficiently and effectively, thereby enhancing productivity and optimizing workflows. This chapter delves into the art and science of scripting with Python, spotlighting areas such as system administration, web browsing automation using Selenium, and the automation of scheduled tasks with cron in Linux environments or its equivalents in other operating systems. Through practical examples and clear explanations, readers will learn how to write scripts that can handle filesystem operations, manage running processes, automate interaction with web pages, and schedule scripts to run at predefined times or intervals. By the end of this chapter, the readers will not only grasp the concepts and techniques but also be able to apply them in real-world scenarios, turning repetitive tasks into automated processes with Python. This knowledge not only bolsters one's toolset for system administration and web tasks but also broadens the horizon into other domains where Python scripts can be a game-changer.

Scripting for System Administration

In the world of technology, efficiency and automation are key. For system administrators, scripts serve as powerful tools to automate routine tasks, manage system resources, and monitor system health. Python, with its simplicity and wide range of libraries, stands out as an excellent language for scripting in system administration. This section delves into how Python can be harnessed to write scripts that streamline system administration tasks.

At the heart of system administration is the need to perform tasks accurately and efficiently. Python scripts enable administrators to automate mundane tasks such as file management, system monitoring, and backup operations. This not only saves time but also reduces the likelihood of human error. The first step in using Python for system administration is understanding the basics of file handling and process management, which are covered extensively in previous chapters.

One common task in system administration is parsing log files. Python's standard library offers several modules such as **re** for regular expressions and **logparser**, making the parsing of log files for error detection and system monitoring a breeze. By automating this task, administrators can proactively address issues before they escalate.

Another critical area is network management. Python's **socket** library facilitates the creation of scripts that can monitor network connections, perform diagnostics, and even automate repairs. Through such scripts, administrators can ensure that network resources remain available and performant. Furthermore, Python's **requests** module allows for easy manipulation of HTTP requests, which is handy for testing web servers and APIs.

Scripting with Python also extends to database administration. Python's **sqlite3** module, for example, enables interaction with SQLite databases. This is particularly useful for managing local databases used by applications or websites. Additionally, Python's ORM libraries such as SQLAlchemy can simplify database operations, making the code more readable and maintainable.

One of the most powerful features of using Python for system administration is its ability to integrate with almost any system, thanks to the vast array of third-party libraries. For example, libraries such as **Paramiko** allow for SSH connections and operations, enabling remote system management within Python scripts.

Automation scripts can sometimes lead to unforeseen issues if not tested thoroughly. Therefore, incorporating error handling and logging within your scripts is crucial. Python's **try-except** blocks and logging module provide the necessary constructs for robust error handling and logging practices, ensuring that your scripts are reliable and maintainable.

Scheduling tasks is another facet where Python scripts shine. By integrating with system schedulers like cron on Linux or Task Scheduler on Windows, Python scripts can be executed at predefined times or intervals. This is particularly useful for tasks such as regular backups, system updates, or periodic cleaning of temporary files.

Security in scripting cannot be overstated. With Python's **hashlib** and **cryptography** modules, scripts can be designed to securely handle sensitive information through encryption and secure hash algorithms. This ensures that scripts dealing with user credentials or confidential data maintain a high level of security.

Python also excels in automating the deployment of software and updates across systems. Using scripts, administrators can manage deployment processes, ensuring that all systems are up-to-date with the latest security patches and features. This automation is especially valuable in environments where downtime must be minimized.

For system administrators looking to manage cloud resources, Python's **boto3** library provides an interface to Amazon Web Services, while **google-cloud-python** offers similar functionality for Google Cloud Platform. These libraries allow for the automation of cloud resource provisioning, monitoring, and management, reflecting the growing trend of cloud computing in system administration.

An inherent advantage of using Python for scripting is its cross-platform nature. Python scripts written for system administration tasks can generally be used across different operating systems with minimal modifications. This universality makes Python an ideal choice for administrators managing heterogeneous environments.

Python's scriptability extends to the automation of user management tasks as well. By scripting user account creation, modification, and deletion, system administrators can efficiently manage user accounts across systems and platforms.

Last but not least, the community around Python offers a plethora of resources for learning and troubleshooting. Whether it's through official documentation, forums, or open-source projects, system administrators can find solutions, share insights, and contribute back to the community, enhancing their skills and the tools at their disposal.

In conclusion, Python stands as a formidable tool in the arsenal of system administration. It offers a balance of simplicity, power, and flexibility, making it ideal for a wide range of system administration tasks. From automating routine maintenance to managing complex systems, Python scripts help system administrators achieve efficiency, accuracy, and reliability in their daily operations. As such, embracing Python scripting not only propels one's career forward but also significantly contributes to the operational excellence of IT environments.

Automating Web Browsing with Selenium

Transitioning from understanding the nuances of Python to applying it in automating mundane or complex tasks creates an exciting phase in any developer's journey. Among these applications, automating web browsing stands out due to its vast utility across different professional and personal projects. This section explores the Selenium WebDriver, a pivotal tool in the realm of browser automation with Python.

Selenium is an open-source framework that enables interaction with web browsers in an automated fashion. It supports various browsers including Chrome, Firefox, and Safari, making it a versatile choice for developers and testers. The power of Selenium lies in its ability to automate testing for web applications, but its utility goes beyond testing to include any task requiring web browser interaction.

Before diving into the technical details, it's essential to set up the environment for Selenium. This process starts with installing the Selenium package in Python, which can be done using pip, Python's package manager. The command ***pip install selenium*** ensures that Selenium is added to your toolkit. However, merely installing the Selenium library isn't enough; you'll also need the appropriate WebDriver for the browser you intend to automate.

WebDrivers are crucial components that act as a link between your Selenium scripts and the web browser. Each major browser requires a different WebDriver, which you must download and place in a directory accessible to your Python scripts. For instance, automating Chrome requires chromedriver, while Firefox needs geckodriver. Ensuring the right setup before jumping into automation is imperative to avoid runtime errors.

Once the setup is complete, you can begin writing Python scripts to interact with web pages. Starting with basic tasks like opening a web page involves importing the Selenium WebDriver module and specifying which browser to automate. Creating a browser instance and using the ***get*** method allows you to navigate to any URL of your choice.

Automation with Selenium isn't limited to navigating web pages; it also includes interacting with web elements. Whether it's filling out forms, clicking buttons, or retrieving data from a website, Selenium provides methods like ***find_element_by_id***, ***find_element_by_name***, and ***find_element_by_xpath*** to locate and manipulate these elements. Understanding how to select elements accurately is key to effective automation.

An essential part of automating web browsing is handling waits and page loads. Websites may not load instantly, and Selenium scripts might attempt to interact with elements that aren't yet available. This issue is tackled through implicit and explicit waits, allowing the script to pause for a specified time or until a certain condition is met, ensuring the elements are interactable.

Moreover, Selenium's capability to manage cookies allows for sessions to be saved and restored, enabling testing scenarios that require authentication or certain preferences to be remembered across browser sessions. This feature is particularly useful for automating tasks on websites where login is required.

Error handling in Selenium scripts also deserves attention. As with any programming task, things might not always go as planned. Elements might not be found, actions might fail, and unexpected pop-ups might appear. Incorporating try-except blocks in your scripts can help manage these uncertainties, making your automation more robust and reliable.

For testing purposes, Selenium integrates well with testing frameworks such as PyTest and unittest. This integration allows for the creation of automated test suites that can run periodically, ensuring the continued functionality of web applications. The ability to run tests in headless mode, where the browser's UI isn't displayed, further facilitates the integration of Selenium tests into continuous integration pipelines.

Exploring advanced features of Selenium unveils even greater possibilities. Taking screenshots, handling browser windows and tabs, and executing JavaScript within the browser context are just a few examples of what can be achieved. These capabilities allow for comprehensive automation and testing strategies that can mimic a wide range of user interactions.

While Selenium is powerful, it's crucial to recognize its limitations. Its reliance on web elements and their properties means that significant changes to a web application's UI can break your scripts. Regular maintenance and updates are often necessary to keep scripts functioning as intended. Additionally, Selenium automates browsers, not directly HTTP requests; for direct web requests, tools like Requests in Python might be more appropriate.

Despite these challenges, automating web browsing with Selenium opens up a world of possibilities. From automating repetitive web tasks to creating complex test suites for web applications, Selenium provides the tools needed to interact with the web in an automated, efficient manner. By harnessing the power of Selenium alongside Python, developers can save time, improve accuracy, and increase the reliability of web interactions and testing procedures.

In conclusion, entering the realm of web automation with Selenium and Python expands one's toolkit, enabling the automation of virtually any web-based task. Whether you're a beginner looking to automate simple tasks or an advanced developer creating intricate automation scripts, Selenium offers the functionality and flexibility to meet a wide array of needs. As you continue to explore the capabilities of Python, integrating Selenium into your projects can significantly enhance your ability to interact with and automate web browsers, pushing the boundaries of what can be achieved with automated scripts.

Scheduling Tasks with Cron and Python

After exploring how Python serves as a powerful tool for automation in various fields, it's crucial to understand how to schedule these automations to run at specified times, thereby increasing efficiency and reliability. This chapter delves into the world of task scheduling with Cron in conjunction with Python scripts, a combination that enables the automation of repetitive tasks without manual intervention.

Cron is a time-based job scheduler in Unix-like operating systems, which uses a crontab (cron table) file to schedule jobs (commands or scripts) to run periodically at fixed times, dates, or intervals. Python scripts, when paired with Cron, can be executed as scheduled tasks, making the automation process seamless and more powerful. This integration is especially useful for system maintenance, monitoring, and regular data processing tasks.

To begin with, understanding the syntax of a crontab file is essential. Each line in this file represents a task and consists of a CRON expression, followed by the command to be executed. The CRON expression is a string comprised of five or six fields: minute, hour, day of the month, month, day of the week, and optionally, year, where each part represents a time unit.

For instance, scheduling a Python script to run daily at midnight would involve adding a line such as **0 0 * * * /usr/bin/python3 /path/to/script.py** to the crontab file. This indicates that the script located at **/path/to/script.py** should execute when the minute is 0 and the hour is 0, effectively, at midnight every day.

Editing the crontab file requires using the **crontab -e** command. This opens the file in the default editor, where new tasks can be defined or existing ones modified. It's critical to ensure the correct Python interpreter path is specified and that the script is executable. Moreover, the context in which cron jobs run might differ from the user's regular environment, which can affect the execution of Python scripts. It's advisable to specify absolute paths for the Python interpreter and script file to mitigate such issues.

Handling output is another crucial aspect of scheduling Python scripts with Cron. By default, Cron sends any output from the script, including errors, to the email address associated with the user account that scheduled the job. However, it's often more practical to redirect this output to files for logging purposes using redirection operators. For example, appending > **/path/to/logfile.log 2>&1** to the end of the crontab line will redirect both standard output and standard error to **/path/to/logfile.log**.

When scheduling tasks, it's also important to consider the environment in which the Python script will run. Environmental variables that are present in the user's session might not be available in the Cron execution environment. To handle this, one can define necessary environment variables directly in the crontab file or ensure the Python script is robust enough to work in a minimal environment.

Precise timing is another area where Cron shows its adaptability. For instance, tasks that need to run on specific days of the week or month can be scheduled with ease. The flexibility in scheduling allows Python scripts to be used in a wider array of applications, from data backups that run in the off-hours to reports that are generated first thing in the morning.

Error handling within Python scripts becomes more significant when scheduled with Cron. Since there isn't an interactive user to respond to prompts or unexpected issues, scripts need to be designed to handle exceptions gracefully and, where possible, resolve issues autonomously or log detailed error information for later analysis.

Monitoring and managing Cron jobs is facilitated through various commands. For instance, **crontab -l** lists all scheduled tasks for the current user, while **crontab -r** removes all scheduled tasks without confirmation, a command to be used with caution.

Security considerations must also be kept in mind. Since Cron jobs often have the same permissions as the user who schedules them, it's essential to ensure that scripts do not unintentionally expose sensitive information or introduce security vulnerabilities.

For more complex scheduling needs, Python itself offers packages, such as *schedule* and *APScheduler*, that provide more flexibility and control than Cron. These packages allow for scheduling tasks from within Python scripts, with more sophisticated scheduling logic than is feasible with Cron expressions alone. Yet, Cron's simplicity and ubiquity make it a valuable tool for many automation tasks.

Integrating Python scripts with Cron leverages the strengths of both tools, offering a robust solution for automating and scheduling tasks. With careful planning and consideration of the execution environment, output handling, and error management, Python scripts scheduled with Cron can perform a wide range of tasks reliably and without direct supervision.

To sum up, mastering Cron and Python in tandem opens up a myriad of possibilities for automating tasks across systems. Whether you're managing server backups, performing regular data analysis, or automating system updates, the combination of Cron's scheduling capabilities with Python's versatility and power is a match that can significantly enhance productivity and operational efficiency.

Chapter 13: Testing Your Python Code

In the relentless pursuit of writing robust and error-free Python code, Chapter 13 serves as a vital checkpoint for developers at all levels of expertise. Testing, often perceived as a daunting or tedious task, is demystified and presented as an integral part of the development process, not merely an afterthought. This chapter embarks on exploring the intricacies of unit testing using the **unittest** framework, a built-in Python module that supports test automation, sharing of setup and shutdown code for tests, aggregation of tests into collections, and the separation of tests from the production code. It emphasizes the philosophy and practicalities of Test-Driven Development (TDD), an advanced programming practice that encourages simple designs and inspires confidence. Through practical examples and clear explanations, readers learn to write tests that improve code quality and ensure functionality meets business requirements before deployment. Furthermore, integration testing best practices are illustrated, showing how individual software modules are combined and tested as a group, ensuring that interactions between parts do not introduce new faults. The focus on real-world applicability, combined with the expository discussions on the strategies and benefits of various testing methodologies, equips practitioners with an arsenal to tackle software errors head-on, fostering a culture of quality and precision in Python programming.

Unit Testing with unittest

As you progress in your journey to become proficient in Python, you'll find that writing reliable and efficient code is not just a matter of skill but also a process that involves thorough testing. Python's standard library includes a powerful module named **unittest**, which is designed for precisely this task. This section delves into the fundamentals of unit testing your Python code with the **unittest** framework, guiding both newcomers and seasoned developers through the intricacies of crafting tests that ensure your code behaves as expected.

Unit testing, at its core, is a method to verify the smallest pieces of testable code against predetermined specifications. In Python, these testable code pieces often manifest as functions or methods within classes. The philosophy here is to create tests for each function or method so that changes to the code can be made confidently without inadvertently introducing bugs elsewhere in the application.

The **unittest** module adopts an OOP (Object-Oriented Programming) approach, which means tests are encapsulated as methods within a class derived from **unittest.TestCase**. This structuring brings out an organized framework that not only helps in writing tests but also in reading and maintaining them.

To start with unit testing, you'd first import the **unittest** module. Then, define a class that inherits from **unittest.TestCase**. Within this class, each test is represented by its own method. By convention, the names of these methods should start with the word 'test', signaling to the **unittest** framework that these methods are tests.

A test case within **unittest** usually follows a basic structure: setup, execution, assertion, and teardown. The setup phase prepares the environment for the test, which often involves preparing objects or data. The execution phase runs the code being tested. The assertion phase then checks if the result obtained from execution matches the expected result. Finally, the teardown phase cleans up any resources used during the test.

The power of the **unittest** module lies in its assertion methods. These are a set of utility methods provided by **unittest.TestCase** to check for and report failures. For example, **assertEqual(a, b)** checks if **a** equals **b**. There are many such methods, each designed for a different kind of assertion, such as **assertTrue()** for verifying boolean conditions, **assertRaises()** for verifying that a specific exception gets raised, etc.

An important aspect of unit testing with **unittest** is the test runner. This is the component that collects all the tests from a test case class (or multiple classes), runs them, and provides the results. Python's **unittest** includes a built-in test runner that, by default, is invoked by calling **unittest.main()**. This scans the file for any **unittest.TestCase** subclasses and automatically runs any method starting with 'test'.

Organizing tests is crucial as you scale up your testing efforts. **unittest** provides features to group related tests within a single test suite. This enables you to organize tests logically and run related tests together. It's particularly useful in larger projects where different components may be tested independently.

Mimicking real-world scenarios is another area where **unittest** shines. Mocking, or the use of dummy objects that simulate real objects within a test environment, is supported natively within **unittest** through the **unittest.mock** module. This allows you to isolate the piece of code being tested and avoid unwanted side effects or the need for complex setup.

It's imperative to write tests that cover multiple scenarios, including typical use cases, edge cases, and error conditions. By doing so, you ensure your application is robust against a wide array of inputs.

Remember, a good test not only checks for the correct output but also that the correct exceptions are raised when invalid input is received.

Another best practice is to aim for a high test coverage. Test coverage refers to the percentage of your codebase tested by unit tests. Though achieving 100% coverage is often impractical, high coverage percentages are advisable. Tools such as Coverage.py can be utilized alongside **unittest** to measure the test coverage of your Python code.

While writing tests, it's also crucial to maintain them. Refactoring tests, updating them according to changes in the codebase, and removing redundant tests ensure that your test suite remains effective and manageable. Remember, the goal of testing is not to make testing harder or slower but to make writing and maintaining reliable code easier.

Integrating unit tests into your development cycle early can have profound benefits. It encourages a deeper understanding of the codebase, highlights potential issues at an earlier stage, and fosters a culture of quality within the development team. This practice, commonly known as Test-Driven Development, starts with tests to drive the design of the code. It's a powerful approach but requires discipline and understanding of the fundamentals of unit testing as discussed.

In conclusion, **unittest** provides a comprehensive framework for unit testing in Python. It supports the creation, organization, execution, and maintenance of tests, promoting software reliability and maintainability. Whether you're a beginner or an experienced developer, incorporating **unittest** into your Python projects can significantly enhance the quality of your code and your productivity as a programmer. Embrace unit testing as an integral part of your development process, and you'll soon reap the benefits of cleaner, more reliable code.

Test-Driven Development (TDD)

Test-Driven Development, or TDD, is a software development approach where tests are written before the actual code. This technique encourages developers to think about the functionality and design of their code beforehand, leading to a more thoughtful and deliberate coding process. It's a cycle commonly described as red-green-refactor: first, you write a test that fails (red), then you implement the minimum amount of code necessary to pass the test (green), and finally, you refactor the code to ensure quality and optimization.

In the context of Python, TDD can significantly enhance the quality of software projects, making the code more robust and maintainable. Given Python's versatility and simplicity, it's an excellent language for those just beginning with TDD. Python's standard library includes the **unittest** framework, providing a solid foundation for writing and executing tests.

The first step in TDD is to write a test for a new function or feature before its implementation. For instance, if you're developing a function to add two numbers, you start by writing a test that checks if the function produces the correct output for given inputs. Initially, this test will fail because the function hasn't been implemented yet. This failure is expected and serves as a baseline for the development process.

After writing the initial test, the next step is to write just enough code to make the test pass. This encourages developers to focus on solving one specific problem at a time, which can lead to cleaner, more understandable code. In our example, you would implement the function to add two numbers in the simplest way possible to pass the test.

Once the test passes, the next phase is refactoring. Refactoring involves modifying the code without changing its external behavior to improve its structure, performance, or readability. Refactoring is a crucial step in TDD, as it allows developers to optimize their code in light of the tests they've written.

TDD has several benefits, one of which is improved code quality. By writing tests first, developers are forced to think through the requirements and edge cases upfront, leading to more thorough coverage and fewer bugs. Furthermore, having a suite of tests makes it easier to refactor and extend the code with confidence, knowing that existing functionality won't break.

Another advantage of TDD is better designed, more modular code. Because TDD encourages writing smallest possible code snippets to pass tests, the resulting code tends to be more focused and modular. This modularity makes the code easier to understand and maintain.

Documentation is another implicit benefit of TDD. The tests you write serve as live documentation for your code. They provide concrete examples of how functions are supposed to be used and what their expected outputs are. This can be incredibly helpful for new team members or when revisiting a codebase after some time.

Starting with TDD can be challenging, especially for beginners. It requires a shift in mindset from writing code first to writing tests first. Initially, it might seem like it slows down the development process. However, the investment in writing tests pays dividends in the long run by reducing bugs and making the code easier to maintain and extend.

It's important to note that TDD doesn't replace traditional testing methods but complements them. Other forms of testing, like integration testing and system testing, are still necessary to ensure the application works as expected from end to end.

Python's dynamic nature and the rich ecosystem of testing tools make it an excellent choice for applying TDD. Tools and frameworks like PyTest offer more features and a more straightforward syntax compared to **unittest**, facilitating a more efficient TDD process.

In practice, applying TDD in Python projects starts with defining the functionality you want to implement. Then, write a test that describes the desired behavior. Run the test to ensure it fails (since the functionality isn't implemented yet), implement the functionality, and then run the test again to ensure it passes. Refactor your code as necessary, making sure all tests still pass after refactoring.

Embracing TDD is a journey. Initially, it may be difficult to resist the urge to dive straight into coding. However, with practice, TDD can become an integral part of your development workflow, leading to more reliable, maintainable, and high-quality Python code.

Finally, TDD fosters a culture of testing within teams, pushing for better practices in software development. It encourages developers to take ownership of their code's quality and integrity from the start, aligning with Python's philosophy of simplicity and elegance. As you progress in your Python journey, integrating TDD into your development process can significantly elevate the robustness and reliability of your software projects.

Integration Testing Best Practices

As we delve into the intricate world of testing Python code, it's essential to recognize the pivotal role that integration testing plays in ensuring our applications function as intended when different modules or services are combined. Unlike unit testing, which isolates and verifies individual components, integration testing focuses on the interactions and interfaces between components, making it a critical step in the software development lifecycle.

One of the foundational best practices in integration testing is to start testing early in the development process. This approach, often referred to as 'shift left,' emphasizes the importance of detecting and addressing integration issues as soon as possible. Doing so not only reduces the time and cost associated with fixing bugs but also helps maintain a high level of code quality throughout the development phase.

Another key practice is to automate your integration tests. Automation can significantly increase the efficiency and reliability of your testing process by enabling you to run tests frequently and consistently without manual intervention. This is particularly valuable in today's fast-paced development environments, where continuous integration and delivery (CI/CD) pipelines rely heavily on automated tests to facilitate rapid, iterative releases.

To further enhance the effectiveness of your integration testing strategy, it's crucial to maintain a clean, well-organized test environment. This involves ensuring that your test data is representative of real-world scenarios and that any external dependencies, such as databases or third-party services, are properly accounted for and managed. Using tools like Docker can help isolate and replicate specific components or services, thereby providing a more controlled and predictable testing environment.

Additionally, prioritize testing the most critical paths of interaction within your application. Identify which components or services are most vital to your application's functionality and start by focusing your testing efforts on these areas. This risk-based approach helps ensure that major issues are discovered early, allowing for smoother and more focused development and testing cycles.

When implementing integration tests, it's also beneficial to adopt a modular approach. Break down your tests into smaller, manageable units that target specific interactions or functionalities. This not only makes your tests easier to write and maintain but also facilitates quicker identification and resolution of issues.

Don't overlook the importance of clear, comprehensive documentation for your integration tests. Proper documentation helps future developers understand the purpose and scope of each test, making it easier for teams to update tests as the application evolves. Moreover, well-documented tests can serve as valuable references during code reviews and debugging sessions.

Performance considerations should also play a role in your integration testing strategy. Be on the lookout for any performance bottlenecks or scalability issues that arise when components interact. Incorporating performance tests into your integration testing can reveal critical insights into how your application behaves under different loads and conditions.

Communication and collaboration among team members are essential in effectively planning and executing integration tests. Developers, testers, and operations personnel should work closely together to define test criteria, share feedback, and address any issues that arise. Foster a culture of openness and continuous improvement, where learning from mistakes and refining processes is encouraged.

Incorporate feedback loops into your integration testing process. Utilize the results of your tests to refine and improve your code, tests, and overall development strategy continually. Tools that provide insights into test coverage and success rates can be invaluable in identifying areas for improvement.

Consider using service virtualization to simulate components or services that are not available or are too costly to include in every test run. This approach can be particularly useful in complex systems with many external dependencies, allowing you to test interactions without the need for the actual production services to be available.

Finally, always be prepared to adapt and evolve your integration testing practices. As your application and its environment change, so too should your testing strategies. Stay informed about new tools, techniques, and best practices in integration testing and be willing to experiment to find what works best for your team and project.

By adhering to these best practices, you can ensure that your integration testing is as effective and efficient as possible. Remember, integration testing is not just a step in the development process; it's an ongoing commitment to quality and reliability in the software you deliver. So, embrace these practices, and let them guide you in creating robust, error-free Python applications that stand the test of time.

Chapter 14: Python for Networking and Security

In this chapter, we delve into Python's powerful capabilities in the realms of networking and security, offering a foundation for those looking to expand their Python toolkit into these essential areas of computing. Starting with socket programming, readers are guided through the basics of how Python can interact with various networking protocols to send and receive data, enabling the creation of client-server applications. This section demystifies the complexities of network communication, illustrating how Python's standard library simplifies these processes: Moving forward, the chapter shifts attention to network automation, a vital skill in managing large networks efficiently. Readers learn to leverage Python scripts to automate repetitive network configuration and management tasks, significantly reducing the margin for error and the time spent on routine operations. Lastly, we explore the introduction to cryptography with Python, emphasizing its importance in securing data transmission across networks. This section provides a primer on how Python can be used to encrypt and decrypt data, ensuring confidentiality and integrity in communication. By the chapter's end, readers will have a solid understanding of how Python tools and libraries can be employed to tackle real-world networking and security challenges, positioning them well for more advanced exploration of these topics.

Socket Programming Basics

As we delve into the realm of Python for networking and security, it is essential to grasp the foundation of socket programming. Sockets provide the communication mechanism between two computers using a network. In Python, the socket module embodies methods to facilitate this kind of communication, allowing for both server and client programming.

At its core, a socket represents the endpoint in a network communication scenario. Python's socket module allows for creating these endpoints, initiating connections, listening for incoming data, and sending information. Understanding sockets is pivotal for anyone aiming to write network applications or perform network automation using Python.

To start with socket programming, one must import the socket module. This module provides access to the BSD socket interface, offering various functions and constants to work with sockets. Creating a socket involves calling the **socket.socket()** function, which returns a socket object. This object can then be configured and used to establish connections.

There are mainly two types of sockets in Python: TCP (Transmission Control Protocol) and UDP (User Datagram Protocol) sockets. TCP sockets establish a reliable and connection-oriented communication pathway, ensuring that data sent from one end is received by the other end. UDP sockets, however, are connectionless and are used in cases where speed is preferred over reliability, such as streaming applications.

A typical TCP server workflow involves creating a socket object, binding it to a specific IP address and port, listening for incoming connections, and then accepting these connections. Upon accepting a connection, the server can read or write data to the client using the connection socket returned by the accept method.

Conversely, a TCP client initiates communication by creating a socket object and then connecting it to a server using the server's IP address and port number. Once the connection is established, the client can send and receive data over the same sockect.

Understanding the client-server model is crucial for socket programming. This model defines how a server provides services to one or more clients, which request and consume these services. A deep dive into this model reveals that robust error handling and concurrency control are vital for developing sophisticated network applications.

Error handling in socket programming can't be overstressed. Network programs must anticipate and gracefully handle errors such as connection timeouts, refused connections, and other network-related anomalies. Python's try-except blocks can be adeptly employed to catch exceptions and mitigate potential crashes of network applications.

Concurrency in server applications denotes the ability to handle multiple clients simultaneously. Python offers several strategies to achieve concurrency, including threading, forking, and asynchronous I/O. Each method serves different use cases, and understanding the nuances of these approaches is key to creating efficient network programs.

Beyond TCP sockets, understanding UDP sockets is equally important. While less reliable than TCP, UDP is faster and simpler, making it suitable for applications where speed trumps reliability. Programming with UDP sockets follows a slightly different approach, mainly due to its connectionless nature.

Given Python's versatility, socket programming extends beyond basic client and server models. Advanced topics such as multicast sockets, non-blocking sockets, and socket options are areas where Python's comprehensive standard library shines, offering functionalities that cater to a broad range of networking requirements.

For those venturing into network automation, mastering socket programming is a stepping stone. Automating network tasks, such as data collection, device configuration, and network testing, can often involve custom socket programming, especially when dealing with legacy systems or specific protocols.

Security in socket programming is another paramount area. Secure sockets layer (SSL) and transport layer security (TLS) are crucial for encrypting data sent over a network. Python's **ssl** module enriches socket programming with methods for wrapping sockets in SSL/TLS, ensuring secure data transmission.

In conclusion, socket programming in Python opens a gateway to network application development. It lays the foundation for more advanced topics in networking and security covered in subsequent chapters. Through practical examples and exercises, one can harness the power of Python to create robust, efficient, and secure network applications. Embracing socket programming is not just about understanding sockets but about unlocking the potential to automate and secure network operations, making it an indispensable skill in the Python programmer's toolkit.

Python for Network Automation

In recent times, network automation has become an essential skill for network engineers and system administrators. The demand for professionals who can automate routine tasks, manage network configurations, and ensure the security of network systems is at an all-time high. Python, with its simplicity and robust library ecosystem, emerges as the language of choice for network automation tasks. In this section, we'll delve into how Python can be leveraged to automate network configurations, manage devices, and much more.

The allure of Python in the context of network automation lies in its libraries such as Netmiko, Paramiko, and Ansible. These libraries provide an abstraction layer on top of SSH (Secure Shell) and other protocols to interact with network devices. This simplifies tasks such as sending commands, retrieving configurations, or automating deployment scripts across multiple devices.

Beyond libraries focused on specific protocols, Python's native libraries play a significant role. For instance, the **socket** library is fundamental for creating TCP/IP clients and servers, facilitating the development of custom network tools or services. Additionally, Python's simplicity allows for quick script development, turning complex tasks into manageable automation scripts that can be deployed across various environments.

Understanding Python's approach to network automation begins with scripting. Scripts are powerful in automating repetitive tasks across a vast network of devices, thereby eliminating human errors and significantly reducing time spent on manual configurations. A simple Python script can log into a device, execute necessary commands, and log out, all within a matter of seconds.

One significant advantage of using Python for network automation is its capability to integrate with existing IT infrastructure. Automation scripts written in Python can seamlessly work with Continuous Integration/Continuous Deployment (CI/CD) pipelines, version control systems, and more. This makes Python not just a tool for network automation but a bridge that connects networking with modern DevOps practices.

For those beginning their journey in network automation with Python, starting with the basics of Python scripting is essential.

Familiarity with Python's syntax, control structures, and libraries will lay a strong foundation. From there, exploring libraries such as Netmiko and understanding their applications in real-world scenarios will be a logical next step.

An example to illustrate Python's power in network automation could be automating the backup of device configurations. With a few lines of Python code, one can write a script that logs into a device, extracts the configuration, and stores it securely. Such automation not only saves time but also adds a layer of reliability to network management practices.

As we delve deeper into network automation, understanding API interactions becomes crucial. Many modern network devices and controllers offer REST APIs for programmatic access. Python's **requests** library simplifies HTTP requests, enabling scripts to interact with these APIs efficiently, opening up a new world of possibilities for network automation.

Security in network automation cannot be overstated. Python supports secure connections, offers libraries for encryption and decryption, and helps in creating secure scripts that protect sensitive information while automating network tasks. This aspect of Python makes it a trustworthy choice for enterprises looking to automate their networks.

Testing plays a fundamental role in network automation. Python's testing frameworks like PyTest can be used to validate the functionality of automation scripts, ensuring they perform as expected across different network scenarios. This is vital for avoiding disruptions in production environments.

Advanced Python topics for network automation include parallel execution and asynchronous programming. These concepts allow scripts to be executed on multiple devices simultaneously, significantly speeding up large-scale operations. Libraries such as **asyncio** are at the forefront of making asynchronous network programming simpler and more efficient.

Finally, transitioning from scripting to developing full-fledged applications for network management is a path many Python developers take. These applications can offer graphical interfaces, real-time monitoring, and advanced configuration controls, all powered by Python's versatility and performance.

In conclusion, Python for network automation is not just about writing scripts. It's about understanding network protocols, security, APIs, and the Python ecosystem to create solutions that are efficient, reliable, and scalable. For beginners, dipping your toes by automating simple tasks can be incredibly rewarding. For advanced users, exploring Python's advanced topics can transform how networks are managed in your organization.

As we move forward into a world where networks become more complex and integral to operations, Python stands as a key tool in the network engineer's toolkit, offering endless possibilities for innovation and efficiency in network automation.

Introduction to Cryptography with Python

Cryptography, the art of secure communication, is a critical field in the modern digital world, covering the confidentiality, integrity, and authenticity of information. Python, with its expansive ecosystem and readable syntax, provides an excellent platform for delving into cryptography. This section introduces the foundational concepts of cryptography and demonstrates how Python can be used to implement these principles.

At its core, cryptography divides into two main types: symmetric and asymmetric encryption. Symmetric encryption uses the same key for both encryption and decryption, making it fast and efficient for many scenarios. Asymmetric encryption, or public-key cryptography, uses a pair of keys, where one key encrypts the data, and a different key is required to decrypt it. This allows for secure communication even if the encryption key is publicly known.

Python's **cryptography** module provides robust support for both types of encryption and is a starting point for anyone looking to implement cryptographic solutions. Installing this package is straightforward with pip, Python's package manager, allowing users to quickly get started with encryption and decryption tasks.

Understanding cryptographic hashes and digital signatures is also essential. Hashes convert data into a fixed-size string of bytes, typically used to ensure data integrity. A digital signature, on the other hand, verifies the authenticity of a message or document. Python's **hashlib** and **cryptography** modules support these functionalities, enabling the creation and verification of hashes and signatures with ease.

Moreover, security is not just about encryption and hashing. Cryptography also involves protocols that ensure secure data transmission over networks. Python's networking capabilities, combined with its cryptographic libraries, allow for the development of secure communication channels, such as SSL/TLS connections.

The practical application of cryptography in Python also extends to file encryption and secure password storage. Encrypting files ensures that sensitive data remains confidential, even if it falls into the wrong hands. When it comes to passwords, cryptographic techniques store them securely, making sure that even if data breaches occur, the passwords remain protected.

Furthermore, Python can be used to build secure authentication systems that use one-time passwords (OTP) or two-factor authentication (2FA), adding an extra security layer beyond traditional password mechanisms. Libraries like **pyotp** make generating and verifying OTPs simple, demonstrating Python's flexibility and power in building secure systems.

One of the critical advantages of using Python for cryptography is its community. An abundance of resources, from documentation to community forums and online courses, are available to help beginners and advanced users alike. Whether it's solving a specific encryption problem or understanding best practices for secure coding, the Python community provides a wealth of knowledge.

For those looking to delve deeper into cryptography with Python, various third-party libraries offer extended functionalities beyond the standard library. These libraries cater to more specialized needs, such as quantum-resistant algorithms or blockchain technologies, showcasing Python's adaptability to evolving cryptographic landscapes.

In addition to theoretical knowledge, practical coding exercises are vital. Implementing cryptographic algorithms by hand, though not recommended for production due to the potential for flaws, serves as an excellent educational tool. It helps in understanding the inner workings of cryptographic protocols and the importance of precise implementation.

The legal and ethical considerations around cryptography cannot be ignored. While encryption serves as a tool for protecting privacy and securing communications, it also poses challenges in law enforcement and regulation. Python programmers venturing into cryptography must stay informed about the legal landscape in their jurisdictions and the ethical implications of their work.

As technology advances, so does the field of cryptography. Keeping up with the latest developments, such as post-quantum cryptography, is crucial. Python, with its ease of picking up new libraries and its active development community, is well-suited for exploring these cutting-edge areas.

In conclusion, Python serves as an excellent gateway into the intricate world of cryptography. Its libraries and community support make it accessible for beginners, yet powerful enough for advanced users to explore complex cryptographic applications. Whether it's for securing personal projects or implementing enterprise-level security systems, Python offers the tools and resources needed to master cryptography.

This introduction to cryptography with Python merely scratches the surface of what's possible. As you progress through this section, you'll gain hands-on experience with coding examples and explore the practical aspects of implementing cryptographic solutions in Python. By the end, you'll have a solid understanding of how to apply Python to achieve confidentiality, integrity, and authenticity in your digital projects.

Chapter 15: Asynchronous Programming in Python

As we delve into Chapter 15, we embark on an exploration of asynchronous programming in Python, a powerful model that allows for more efficient execution of I/O-bound and high-level structured network code. Asynchronous programming is a method where tasks are executed without blocking the main thread of execution, enabling programs to handle tens of thousands of concurrent connections, which is ideal for IO-bound and high-latency activities such as Web API calls, database operations, and file I/O. At the heart of asynchronous programming in Python lies the AsyncIO library, which provides the infrastructure for writing single-threaded concurrent code using coroutines, event loops, and futures. We will journey through the concept of event loops, which serve as the cornerstone of asynchronous execution, and coroutines, a type of function that allows for concurrency and parallelism. Additionally, we'll touch on making asynchronous HTTP requests and interacting with web APIs, which are common use cases in modern web development and application programming. Asynchronous programming in Python not only aids in writing non-blocking code but also in creating more responsive applications that are capable of handling a high volume of requests and operations. By mastering asynchronous programming, developers can significantly optimize the performance and scalability of their Python applications.

Understanding AsyncIO

As we delve into the world of asynchronous programming in Python, AsyncIO stands out as a pivotal component that revolutionizes how Python handles asynchronous operations. This powerful library enables the writing, execution, and management of asynchronous tasks, allowing for scalable and efficient handling of I/O-bound and high-level structured network code.

AsyncIO, introduced in Python 3.4, is part of the standard library, which signifies its importance and integration within Python's ecosystem. It's built on the principles of event loops, coroutines, futures, and tasks. Together, these form the backbone of asynchronous programming in Python, enabling developers to write cleaner, non-blocking code that's both efficient and maintainable.

An event loop, in the context of AsyncIO, is the cornerstone that drives the execution of asynchronous tasks. It runs in a loop, waiting for and dispatching events to the appropriate handler. Programmers can leverage event loops to concurrently run tasks, gather results, and manage asynchronous operations—all within a single thread.

Coroutines, a feature significantly enhanced by the AsyncIO library, are special functions designed to handle the 'awaitables' in asynchronous operations. They allow you to pause the function execution at any await expression and resume it at a later point, thus enabling non-blocking asynchronous execution of code.

Understanding the distinction between synchronous and asynchronous execution models is crucial. In essence, synchronous operations block commands until the task at hand is completed, whereas asynchronous operations allow a program to handle other tasks while waiting for other operations to complete. This non-blocking nature of asynchronous programming is what makes AsyncIO so powerful for network and I/O-bound operations.

AsyncIO provides a framework for developing asynchronous network applications. Being able to handle thousands of connections in a single thread significantly boosts efficiency and performance, especially in web applications, data processing, and networking programs.

The async/await syntax introduced in Python 3.5 has further simplified the way asynchronous code is written. By marking a function with the async keyword, it becomes a coroutine, signifying that it can be paused and resumed. The await keyword is used to pause the execution of a coroutine until the awaited task completes, freeing up the event loop to execute other tasks concurrently.

Futures and tasks in AsyncIO are foundational for scheduling asynchronous operations. A Future is an object that represents an eventual result of asynchronous operations. A Task is a subclass of Future that wraps a coroutine, making it schedulable for execution. Understanding these objects is key to mastering AsyncIO.

To truly leverage the power of AsyncIO, one must grasp how to create and manage event loops, structure coroutines correctly, and utilize futures and tasks. This involves understanding how to write asynchronous functions, schedule them for execution, and retrieve their results upon completion—all of which are crucial skills in asynchronous programming.

One of the common challenges faced by developers when working with AsyncIO is error handling. Unlike synchronous code, where errors can be caught and handled directly, asynchronous code requires a different approach due to its non-linear execution flow. Learning to effectively handle exceptions and errors in asynchronous code is essential for building robust applications with AsyncIO.

Another important aspect to consider is the integration of AsyncIO with existing synchronous code. Often, applications are built with a mix of synchronous and asynchronous functions. Understanding how to bridge these two paradigms seamlessly is critical for the development of efficient and effective software applications.

Performance considerations are paramount when working with asynchronous code. While AsyncIO can significantly improve the performance of I/O-bound applications, it's essential to understand its impact on CPU-bound tasks. Developers must be adept at profiling and optimizing asynchronous Python applications to ensure optimal performance.

Testing asynchronous code presents its own set of challenges. The non-blocking nature of async/await constructs requires a different approach to testing, often involving the use of specific frameworks and tools designed for asynchronous testing. Developing effective testing strategies for AsyncIO applications is crucial for ensuring code reliability and functionality.

In conclusion, mastering AsyncIO is a journey that requires understanding its core concepts—event loops, coroutines, futures, and tasks—alongside developing skills in error handling, performance optimization, and asynchronous testing. Embracing AsyncIO opens up a world of possibilities for developing high-performance, scalable, and efficient Python applications, particularly in the domains of web development, networking, and data processing.

As we move forward into more specialized aspects of asynchronous programming in Python, including event loops and coroutines, keep in mind the foundational knowledge of AsyncIO. This understanding is crucial for navigating the asynchronous features and capabilities of Python, ensuring you can write, debug, and optimize asynchronous Python code with confidence and precision.

Event Loops and Coroutines

The concepts of event loops and coroutines form the backbone of asynchronous programming in Python. To truly understand and harness the power of Python's async features, it's crucial to grasp these two core ideas. They allow developers to write code that's non-blocking and efficient, especially valuable in IO-bound tasks such as web requests, database operations, and file handling.

At its essence, an event loop is a programming construct that waits for and dispatches events or messages in a program. It works by repeatedly collecting events from the application and executing the corresponding callbacks. Think of it as a manager that handles and delegates tasks asynchronously. Python's *asyncio* library provides a robust foundation for writing asynchronous programs through its event loop.

Coroutines, on the other hand, are a broader concept that includes the async/await syntax introduced in Python 3.5. They are specialized versions of Python generators, designed to be paused and resumed, and are the secret sauce that makes asynchronous programming in Python both possible and relatively easy. When a coroutine yields control, it allows the event loop to continue running other tasks, only resuming the coroutine once the event it's waiting on is completed.

Integrating these concepts, *asyncio* enables developers to write highly efficient and scalable network-oriented programs. With *asyncio*, Python developers can efficiently run and manage thousands of network connections, each represented as a coroutine, without resorting to traditional threading or multiprocessing approaches.

To see these ideas in action, consider a simple example involving network IO. Traditionally, making a network request would block the execution of your program until the request returns a response. This is not ideal for performance, especially when dealing with multiple requests. Enter coroutines.

With *asyncio* and coroutines, you can initiate a network request and while waiting for the response, the event loop can perform other tasks. Once the response is ready, the event loop resumes the coroutine from where it was paused. This approach allows for concurrent execution without the complexity of threads, leading to more readable and maintainable code.

But how do you actually use these tools in your code? It starts with the async keyword, which you can use to define a coroutine. For instance, defining an asynchronous function simply involves prefacing the *def* keyword with *async*. Within async functions, you can await on functions that are capable of suspending execution until the awaited task completes. Here, the await keyword is followed by an object known as an awaitable – typically another coroutine.

```
Consider the asynchronous equivalent of the
sleep function from the
asyncio library:
import asyncio
async def main():
print('Hello')
await asyncio.sleep(1)
print('World')
asyncio.run(main())
```

This simple program demonstrates the non-blocking nature of async functions. When *asyncio.sleep()* is called, it doesn't block the entire program but merely yields execution back to the event loop, allowing other tasks to run during the wait period.

What truly elevates the power of event loops and coroutines is their scalability. In a web application that handles thousands of concurrent connections, traditional synchronous code would need to use threads to achieve concurrency, which is resource-intensive and can introduce complex bugs due to shared state and race conditions. Async IO, with its event-driven nature, sidesteps these issues, allowing for a more straightforward and efficient concurrency model.

Moreover, the *asyncio* library is not just limited to handling IO operations. It provides a rich set of features including support for asynchronous file operations, subprocess management, queues, and synchronization primitives similar to those found in traditional threading modules but designed explicitly for use with coroutines.

While the concepts of event loops and coroutines might seem daunting at first, especially to those new to asynchronous programming, they unlock a higher level of efficiency and scalability in Python programs. With practice, these constructs become powerful tools in a developer's arsenal, enabling them to write highly concurrent programs that are both efficient and maintainable.

Asynchronous programming in Python, facilitated by event loops and coroutines, represents a significant shift from traditional, linear ways of thinking about code execution. It allows developers to take full advantage of modern computer architectures, particularly in IO-bound and high-concurrency applications.

Finally, it is worth noting that while *asyncio* is a robust solution for asynchronous programming in Python, it isn't a silver bullet. It's most beneficial when used in the right context, particularly for IO-bound tasks. CPU-bound tasks, which require significant computation, may not see the same level of benefit from an asynchronous approach and might be better suited for parallel execution strategies like multiprocessing.

In conclusion, event loops and coroutines stand at the heart of asynchronous programming in Python, offering a model of concurrency that is both powerful and accessible. Understanding and applying these concepts allows developers to write efficient, non-blocking, and high-performing applications, particularly in network-oriented or IO-bound domains.

Asynchronous HTTP Requests and Web APIs

In the modern web, the ability to perform asynchronous HTTP requests is a critical skill for developers. Using Python, one can efficiently manage data exchange between clients and servers without blocking the execution of a program. This is particularly important when developing applications that consume or provide data through Web APIs.

Asynchronous programming in Python, especially in the context of HTTP requests and Web APIs, revolves around the use of libraries such as **asyncio** and **aiohttp**. These libraries enable the handling of asynchronous operations, allowing developers to run concurrent HTTP requests and operations without freezing the user interface or backend processes.

The concept of asynchronous HTTP requests can be somewhat counterintuitive at first. Traditionally, HTTP requests are made synchronously, meaning that the program will halt its execution until the server responds. In contrast, asynchronous requests send off a request to the server and then proceed with other tasks until the server's response arrives, at which point a callback function can process the response. This model is highly efficient for web scraping, APIs consumption, and handling simultaneous connections to multiple services.

To implement asynchronous HTTP requests in Python, one begins with the **asyncio** library, which provides the framework for running asynchronous tasks. **Asyncio** uses event loops to manage and distribute tasks efficiently. An important concept within **asyncio** is the coroutine, a special function that can pause and resume its execution without losing its state, thus enabling non-blocking IO operations.

The **aiohttp** library further extends **asyncio**'s capabilities, specifically designed for handling HTTP requests and servers. It leverages **asyncio**'s event loop to send and receive HTTP requests asynchronously. With **aiohttp**, one can perform GET, POST, and other methods of HTTP requests, handle cookies, sessions, and use SSL for secure connections, all within an asynchronous execution model.

Consider a practical example where you need to gather data from several Web APIs simultaneously. Using synchronous requests could dramatically increase the total execution time, as each request would block the program flow until a response is received. However, by implementing asynchronous requests with **asyncio** and **aiohttp**, you could dispatch all requests almost at the same time, working on different tasks while waiting for responses, and thus complete the job much faster.

When developing applications that interact with Web APIs, understanding the HTTP protocol is essential. HTTP status codes, request methods, headers, and body payloads must be handled correctly to ensure successful communication between the client and server. Asynchronous programming does not change the fundamentals of HTTP but allows for more efficient interactions.

One common challenge in asynchronous programming is error handling. When a request fails in a synchronous program, it's usually straightforward to catch the error and respond accordingly. In an asynchronous environment, errors can occur at any stage in the execution flow, and managing them requires careful structuring of try-except blocks around asynchronous tasks.

It is also crucial to consider the implications of asynchronous programming on the design of web applications. For instance, user interfaces must be responsive and capable of handling real-time updates, which asynchronous HTTP requests can facilitate. Backend systems, on the other hand, benefit from asynchronous processing by being able to handle high volumes of requests or tasks without being tied up waiting for single operations to complete.

From a scalability perspective, asynchronous programming can greatly enhance the performance of web applications. Servers that utilize asynchronous IO can serve more requests with fewer resources, leading to cost-effective scaling solutions. This is particularly advantageous in cloud computing environments where resources are flexible but can incur significant costs.

Finally, integrating asynchronous HTTP requests and Web APIs into a Python application involves more than just programming. It requires an understanding of the operational environment, including networking considerations, latency, bandwidth limitations, and the behavior of external services. These factors can greatly influence the design and performance of asynchronous operations.

In summary, the incorporation of asynchronous HTTP requests and Web APIs in Python programming represents a significant advancement in how developers interact with the web. It not only enhances efficiency and scalability but also opens up a world of possibilities for creating more interactive and responsive applications. By mastering asynchronous programming techniques, developers can take full advantage of the powerful capabilities of Python in the modern web landscape.

For those embarking on this journey, it is recommended to start with simple tasks and progressively tackle more complex asynchronous operations. Documentation and community resources for libraries like **asyncio** and **aiohttp** are invaluable in this learning process. With practice and dedication, mastering asynchronous programming in Python will become an attainable and rewarding goal.

As we proceed in this book, we will delve deeper into practical examples and advanced features of asynchronous programming. The knowledge gained in this section will serve as a foundation for understanding how to efficiently interact with Web APIs and handle HTTP requests in a non-blocking manner. The ability to execute asynchronous operations effectively is a key skill in the toolkit of modern Python developers.

Chapter 16: Web Scraping with Python

In the current chapter, we dive into the fascinating world of web scraping using Python—a powerful tool for extracting information from websites. Web scraping is a critical skill for many professionals, including data scientists and analysts, who rely on readily available web data for research, analysis, and decision-making. Python, with its rich ecosystem of libraries and frameworks, offers an unparalleled environment for web scraping. We start by exploring the legal considerations of web scraping, ensuring that readers understand the importance of respecting copyright and terms of use of online resources. The discussion then shifts to practical techniques and tools, notably Beautiful Soup and the Scrapy framework, which simplify the process of extracting data from the web. Managing the data once it's been extracted is also covered, providing a comprehensive guide to storing, processing, and using web data effectively. This chapter equips readers with the knowledge to harness the power of web scraping, allowing them to unlock new data sources and gain insights previously hidden in the vast expanses of the web.

The Legalities of Web Scraping

As we transition from understanding the technical intricacies of Python to its application in web scraping, a crucial topic that often surfaces is the legal landscape surrounding web scraping practices. It's imperative for beginners, intermediate coders, software developers, and data scientists alike to navigate these waters with caution, understanding that the legal framework can significantly affect how and what data can be legally extracted from websites.

Web scraping, in its essence, involves extracting data from websites. This can range from simple tasks like retrieving current weather data to more complex operations such as gathering consumer reviews from e-commerce platforms. However, the legality of scraping varies based on several factors including the source, method, and intent of data extraction.

First and foremost, it's essential to note that not all data on the internet is freely available for scraping. Websites often have terms of service (ToS) that explicitly prohibit automated access or data extraction. These ToS are legally binding agreements, and violating them can lead to legal action against the scraper. Therefore, a fundamental step before initiating any scraping project is to carefully review the website's ToS.

Another significant legal consideration is the Computer Fraud and Abuse Act (CFAA) in the United States, which makes it illegal to access computer systems without authorization. Some court cases have interpreted web scraping as a form of unauthorized access, especially if it involves circumventing any form of access control or ignoring a site's robots.txt file. The robots.txt is a file hosted by websites that specifies how and what parts of the site can be crawled by automated agents, including scrapers.

Beyond the CFAA, there are copyright issues to consider. The data you scrape, even if publicly accessible, may be protected by copyright laws. This doesn't mean you can't scrape any data, but the use of scraped data, especially for commercial purposes, can infringe on copyright owners' rights. It's advisable to focus on data that is not copyrighted or to seek permission from copyright holders when necessary.

The European Union's General Data Protection Regulation (GDPR) adds another layer of complexity, especially concerning the scraping of personal data. The GDPR requires explicit consent from individuals before their personal data can be processed. Scraping websites that hold personal information of EU citizens without consent can lead to hefty fines and legal challenges.

Data privacy cannot be overlooked either. Even if legally scraped, mishandling or insecure storage of sensitive data can breach privacy laws, leading to legal repercussions. Responsible handling and ethical considerations should always be at the forefront when processing and storing scraped data.

In certain jurisdictions, specific laws may cover web scraping activities. It's crucial to be aware of and compliant with any local laws and regulations that apply to web scraping projects. Ignorance of the law is often not considered a viable defense in case of legal action.

To mitigate legal risks, many developers and companies opt for APIs provided by websites for data retrieval. These APIs are offered under specific terms and conditions that, when adhered to, offer a legal avenue for data extraction. They typically provide a more straightforward and efficient method for accessing data without the complexities and risks associated with direct scraping.

With the legal framework in mind, it's also important to consider ethics. Just because data can be scraped legally doesn't always mean it should be. Respect for individuals' privacy and the intention behind data usage are critical ethical considerations. Strive to be transparent about how you use scraped data and consider the impact of your scraping activities on the targeted websites and the individuals whose data you may be collecting.

When designing web scraping solutions, employing techniques to minimize the impact on the target website can not only help with legal and ethical considerations but also improve relations with website owners. This includes respecting the robots.txt file, spacing out requests to avoid overloading the server, and identifying your scraping bot accurately via the User-Agent string to allow website owners the option to block or allow your scraper as they see fit.

Documentation and record-keeping can also play a substantial role in the legalities of web scraping. Keeping detailed logs of your scraping activities, including when and what you scrape, can provide necessary documentation in case questions regarding compliance arise.

Finally, consulting with legal professionals who specialize in cyber law can provide valuable insights and guidance tailored to specific scraping projects. They can help navigate the complex web of laws and regulations to ensure that your scraping activities are both effective and compliant with relevant legal statutes.

In conclusion, while web scraping is a powerful tool for data extraction and analysis, it's surrounded by a complex legal framework. Understanding and respecting these legal boundaries, coupled with ethical considerations, can ensure that your scraping projects are both successful and legally compliant. As we delve into the technical aspects of web scraping with Python in the following sections, keep these legalities in mind as they form the foundation on which responsible and effective web scraping practices are built.

Thus, as we proceed to explore the technicalities of using libraries like Beautiful Soup and Scrapy for web scraping in Python, carrying forward the understanding of the legal framework is paramount. This ensures not just the success but also the legality of your data collection efforts, allowing you to leverage web scraping's full potential ethically and responsibly.

Beautiful Soup and Scrapy Framework

Gleaning data from the web is a task that has become commonplace in the realms of data science, market research, and software development. However, the intricacies involved in web scraping are numerous, with challenges ranging from navigating HTML structures to managing dynamic content loading via JavaScript. In this context, Python offers robust solutions, notably through the Beautiful Soup and Scrapy frameworks, which serve as powerful tools for web scraping exercises.

Beautiful Soup stands out for its ease of use and its ability to turn an HTML document into a complex tree of Python objects. This transformation makes it straightforward for developers to navigate and search the parse tree, extract text, and even modify the tree if needed. Its simplicity allows beginners to quickly grasp web scraping concepts and start extracting data with only a few lines of code. Novices will appreciate how Beautiful Soup minimizes the learning curve associated with web scraping.

On the other hand, Scrapy provides a more comprehensive web crawling and scraping framework that allows for scraping a website and extracting the data on a much larger scale. Its architecture is built for speed and efficiency, catering to the needs of developers looking to execute more complex web scraping tasks. Scrapy excels in projects where web crawlers need to follow links and gather data from multiple pages or even multiple sites. It is particularly favored for its capabilities in handling requests, a fundamental feature for dealing with large volumes of data.

One of the significant advantages of using Beautiful Soup is its compatibility with various parsers like lxml and html5lib, which means developers can choose the most appropriate parser for their specific project needs. This flexibility can be crucial in handling different types of web content and structures.

Scrapy's built-in support for outputting scraped data into various formats such as CSV, XML, or JSON is a testament to its utility in the data extraction process. This feature simplifies the task of data analysts and scientists who need to process and analyze large datasets extracted from the web.

For beginners, starting with Beautiful Soup might seem more manageable due to its simpler syntax and direct approach to accessing HTML content. Tackling individual pages and extracting specific data points can be achieved with minimal fuss, making it an excellent starting point for those new to web scraping.

Conversely, professionals or those with a bit more experience under their belt might lean towards Scrapy due to its scalability and the fact that it can handle complex scraping tasks. Scrapy's middleware support and its ability to manage a vast amount of data simultaneously make it stand out for large-scale projects.

Both frameworks are well-documented, offering extensive resources for learning and troubleshooting. Community forums and discussions also provide an invaluable resource for developers encountering unique challenges or seeking optimization techniques for their scraping scripts.

Security is a facet of web scraping that can't be overlooked. Both Beautiful Soup and Scrapy come with measures to respect robots.txt policies, ensuring that your scraping activities remain ethical and within legal boundaries. Understanding how to use these frameworks responsibly is paramount, especially in light of increasing web security and privacy concerns.

Efficiency in web scraping isn't just about the speed of data retrieval but also about minimizing the load on web servers. Scrapy's asynchronous requests feature is designed to handle this delicately, making it possible to scrape data without overwhelming server resources. This approach not only fosters good practices but also ensures that web scraping activities are less likely to be blocked by web administrators.

While Beautiful Soup is incredibly efficient for scraping static websites, Scrapy shines when dealing with dynamic content. Thanks to its built-in support for handling JavaScript, Scrapy can extract data from web pages that rely heavily on AJAX calls for content loading. This capability is crucial for scraping modern web applications that load content dynamically.

Integration capabilities of both frameworks with other Python libraries extend their usefulness. For instance, scraping data with Beautiful Soup or Scrapy and then analyzing it with pandas or NumPy makes for a powerful combination for data scientists. This seamless integration with the Python ecosystem enhances the overall productivity of data extraction and analysis projects.

Education and learning are pivotal aspects of both frameworks. Tutorials and guidebooks are abundantly available, providing step-by-step instructions on deploying Beautiful Soup and Scrapy for web scraping projects. These learning materials are crafted to cater to various skill levels, from beginners to advanced users, ensuring a comprehensive understanding of web scraping principles and practices.

The dynamic nature of the web demands tools that can adapt and evolve. Both Beautiful Soup and Scrapy are actively maintained, with regular updates introducing new features and improvements. This ongoing development ensures that developers have access to the most efficient and effective tools for web scraping, regardless of the shifting landscapes of web technologies.

In conclusion, web scraping with Python is made significantly easier and more accessible through the Beautiful Soup and Scrapy frameworks. Each offers unique advantages that cater to different needs, from simple data extraction tasks to complex web crawling projects. The choice between Beautiful Soup and Scrapy ultimately depends on the specific requirements of the project and the skill level of the developer. With their powerful features, extensive documentation, and active communities, both frameworks are indispensable tools in the arsenal of anyone looking to harness the power of web scraping with Python.

Managing Data Extracted from the Web

In the previous sections, we've explored how to harness the power of Python for web scraping, focusing on tools like Beautiful Soup and Scrapy. As we transition from the mechanics of data extraction to what follows, the emphasis shifts towards the crucial aspect of managing this data. Effectively handling the extracted data not only ensures a streamlined workflow but also magnifies the insights we can derive from the data.

When data is harvested from the web, it often comes in raw, unstructured formats that may not be immediately usable for analysis or application development. The foremost step in managing this data is cleaning it. Data cleaning involves removing extraneous parts that are not relevant to your goals, such as HTML tags when you've extracted textual content or filtering out incomplete datasets that might skew your analysis.

Once the data is cleaned, the next step involves storing it in a manner that supports easy access and analysis. For many applications, this can mean saving the data in structured files like CSV or JSON. Python's rich ecosystem provides robust libraries such as Pandas, which not only helps in storing data but also offers extensive functionalities for data manipulation and analysis.

However, when dealing with large datasets or data that needs frequent updates, storing in files might not be the most efficient approach. This is where databases come into play. Python interacts seamlessly with a variety of databases, be it SQL-based databases like MySQL or SQLite, or NoSQL databases like MongoDB. Choosing the right database usually depends on the project requirements, where considerations might include the complexity of the data, scalability needs, and the query performance.

Further, the realm of data management is not limited to storage and cleaning. Effective data governance practices are crucial. This includes version control systems for data, which can be particularly useful in collaborative environments enabling teams to track changes and manage different versions of the dataset seamlessly.

Another significant aspect of managing web-extracted data is ensuring its integrity and security. Sensitive information needs to be protected, and appropriate measures should be in place to prevent unauthorized access. Python offers numerous libraries and modules for encryption and secure data storage, enabling developers and data scientists to safeguard sensitive information effectively.

Additionally, data validation plays a pivotal role in managing data extracted from the web. Python's flexible nature allows users to leverage regex (regular expressions), custom functions, or even third-party libraries to validate input data, ensuring that it meets the predetermined standards and formats before further processing.

Moreover, in the context of big data and data science, managing data includes the crucial step of data transformation. This might involve converting data formats, enriching or merging datasets, and pre-processing steps like normalization or feature engineering to prepare the data for machine learning models.

Data visualization also forms a part of data management, offering an intuitive understanding of the data, which textual data often cannot provide. Python's visualization libraries like Matplotlib and Seaborn can turn the extracted data into graphical representations, providing insights at a glance and making it easier to spot trends, outliers, or patterns.

Automation in managing data can also significantly enhance productivity. Python scripts can automate various tasks, from the regular extraction of data, cleaning, updating databases, to generating reports or triggering alerts based on specific data changes or thresholds. Such automation can save valuable time and resources, particularly in environments where data is continuously evolving.

Efficient data management is not only about handling the present needs but also about anticipating future requirements. Scalability is a key consideration, especially for web-based applications or data-driven projects poised for growth. Python's scalability and the plethora of libraries available make it a suitable choice for projects that might start small but are expected to scale up.

Lastly, documentation and metadata management are crucial components of a comprehensive data management strategy. Documenting the data extraction process, storage formats, and any transformations or analysis performed on the data ensures transparency and reproducibility, which is essential in both academic and commercial settings.

In conclusion, managing data extracted from the web involves a multifaceted approach that encompasses cleaning, storing, securing, validating, transforming, visualizing, and documenting the data. Python, with its rich ecosystem, provides the tools and libraries necessary to effectively manage this data, supporting a range of applications from web development to data science. As we delve into more specific uses and technologies in the following chapters, it's important to remember that at the heart of these advancements lies the fundamental practice of robust data management.

As we move forward in this book, we'll explore more specialized applications and techniques that build upon these data management foundations, integrating Python's capabilities with modern web technologies, data science methodologies, and beyond. With a solid understanding of how to manage data extracted from the web, readers are well-equipped to tackle more complex challenges and opportunities that lie ahead in their Python journey.

Chapter 17: Python and the Cloud

Entering the realm of cloud computing opens up a vast landscape of possibilities for Python developers. This chapter delves into how Python's flexibility and simplicity make it an ideal companion for cloud-based applications, from automating infrastructure to analyzing vast data lakes. We start by exploring the AWS SDK for Python, known as Boto3, which acts as a gateway for automating AWS cloud services. Not only does it allow for the management of AWS resources directly from Python scripts, but it also simplifies complex cloud operations. We'll then transition to discussing the deployment of Python applications on the cloud, covering the various cloud providers and the PaaS (Platform as a Service) offerings that support Python. This includes how to prepare your Python applications for cloud deployment, considering factors such as scalability, security, and maintenance. Lastly, we touch upon serverless computing with Python, examining how to build and deploy microservices and event-driven functions that scale on-demand without the overhead of managing servers. By the end of this chapter, you'll have a solid foundation for leveraging Python in the cloud to build scalable, efficient, and robust applications, further broadening the horizon of your Python programming capabilities.

Working with AWS SDK for Python (Boto3)

Amazon Web Services (AWS) offers a robust cloud computing platform that can scale with the needs of any project, from a simple blog application to a high-traffic, global service. For Python developers, AWS provides a powerful tool called Boto3, the AWS SDK for Python. Boto3 allows Python developers to create, configure, and manage AWS services directly from Python scripts. This section explores the basics of Boto3, how to set it up, and examples of how to use it to interact with AWS services.

To get started with Boto3, the first step is installing the package. This can be easily done using pip, Python's package installer. Simply run **pip install boto3** in your command line interface, and the SDK will be installed in your Python environment, making it ready for import and use in your scripts.

The next step after installing Boto3 is to configure your AWS credentials. AWS uses these credentials to authenticate your requests and manage access to your resources. You can set up your credentials in several ways, but a common approach is to use the AWS CLI tool and execute **aws configure**. This command prompts you to enter your Access Key ID, Secret Access Key, and default region, which are then stored in a configuration file used by Boto3.

With Boto3 installed and your AWS credentials configured, you're ready to start scripting. A fundamental concept to understand when working with Boto3 is the difference between clients and resources. Clients provide a low-level service access and map closely to the underlying AWS API. Resources, on the other hand, provide a higher-level, object-oriented interface. Most tasks can be accomplished using either, but resources are usually easier to work with.

To illustrate how Boto3 can be utilized, let's consider an example where we list all S3 buckets in an AWS account. Using the client interface, the code snippet would look something like this:

```
import boto3
s3_client = boto3.client('s3')
```

```
buckets = s3_client.list_buckets()
for bucket in buckets['Buckets']:
print(bucket['Name'])
```

Similarly, to perform the same task using the resource interface, the code is slightly more intuitive:

```
import boto3
s3_resource = boto3.resource('s3')
for bucket in s3_resource.buckets.all():
print(bucket.name)
```

These examples highlight Boto3's versatility and how it provides multiple ways to interact with AWS services. Your choice between client and resource interfaces should be guided by your specific needs and the complexity of the task at hand.

One of the strengths of Boto3 is its coverage of AWS services. From launching new EC2 instances to modifying an DynamoDB table, Boto3 has you covered. However, this breadth of service coverage means that mastering Boto3 can be a challenge. A practical approach is to start with the official AWS documentation for Boto3, which provides detailed guides and reference material for all AWS services.

Another crucial aspect when working with Boto3 is handling errors. AWS operations can fail for various reasons, such as network issues or incorrect permissions. Boto3 uses exceptions to signal such problems. Understanding and properly handling these exceptions in your code is key to building robust and reliable applications.

Last but not least, security is paramount when interacting with AWS services through Boto3. Always adhere to the best practices for securing AWS credentials, such as using IAM roles and not hard-coding credentials in your scripts. Also, be mindful of the permissions granted to your AWS account, applying the principle of least privilege to minimize risk.

As a hands-on way to learn Boto3, consider tackling a project that solves a real-world problem. For example, you could write a script that automatically backs up files to an S3 bucket, or a more complex application that uses multiple AWS services. Such projects not only improve your understanding of Boto3 but also deepen your knowledge of cloud computing with AWS.

Throughout your journey with Boto3, you'll discover that it's a powerful ally in the cloud, enabling you to programatically manage a vast array of AWS services. Its extensive documentation, active community, and the fact that it's constantly updated with new features and services make Boto3 an invaluable tool for Python developers looking to leverage the cloud.

In summary, working with AWS SDK for Python opens up a multitude of possibilities for automating and enhancing your cloud-based applications. By mastering Boto3, you not only gain the ability to interact with AWS services in a pythonic way but also set the stage for building scalable and efficient cloud solutions.

Deploying Python Applications on the Cloud

Transitioning from developing Python applications on a local environment to deploying them on the cloud represents a significant leap towards scalability, reliability, and accessibility. This chapter aims to bridge the knowledge gap for Python developers of all skill levels, offering a comprehensive guide to cloud deployment. Deploying applications on the cloud not only broadens the accessibility of the application but also offers the flexibility to manage resources efficiently.

The first step in this journey involves selecting a cloud service provider. The cloud computing market is dominated by giants like

Amazon Web Services (AWS), Google Cloud Platform (GCP), and Microsoft Azure. Each platform offers Python SDKs that simplify the process of integrating your Python application with cloud resources. When choosing a provider, consider factors like cost, scalability, supported services, and the learning curve.

Once you've selected a cloud service provider, the next step is to acquaint yourself with the cloud environment. Cloud platforms typically offer a range of services, from virtual machines to managed databases, and understanding the ecosystem is crucial for effectively deploying and managing your Python applications. Tutorials and documentation provided by cloud services are excellent starting points to gain familiarity with the environment.

Containerization is a popular strategy for deploying Python applications. Containers encapsulate the application and its dependencies, ensuring consistency across different environments. Docker, a platform for developing, shipping, and running applications inside containers, integrates well with Python. Learning Docker and container orchestration tools like Kubernetes will significantly ease the deployment process.

Serverless computing represents another paradigm in cloud deployment, abstracting away the underlying infrastructure. AWS Lambda, Google Cloud Functions, and Azure Functions allow developers to run Python code in response to events without managing servers. Serverless computing is particularly suited for applications with variable workloads, as it offers automatic scaling and pay-per-use pricing models.

Deploying a Python web application often involves working with web frameworks like Django or Flask. These frameworks offer extensive support for cloud deployments, with tutorials and plugins specifically tailored for various cloud platforms. Understanding the deployment options and configurations within your framework of choice is essential for a smooth transition to the cloud.

Cloud storage and databases are critical components of most applications, and Python offers libraries like Boto3 for AWS, google-cloud-storage for GCP, and azure-storage-blob for Azure to interact with cloud storage services. Similarly, Python ORMs like SQLAlchemy can interact with managed database services, making database operations seamless and efficient.

Security is paramount when deploying applications on the cloud. Ensure that your application adheres to best practices, such as using secure connections (HTTPS), managing credentials securely, and complying with data protection regulations. Cloud providers offer tools and services to enhance security, which should be explored and integrated into your deployment process.

Monitoring and logging are essential for maintaining the health of your deployed application. Cloud platforms offer monitoring services that provide insights into application performance and usage patterns. Logging, on the other hand, helps in troubleshooting and understanding the application's runtime behavior. Python's logging module, along with cloud-specific logging services, can be utilized to set up comprehensive logging.

Automating the deployment process can save time and reduce the risk of human errors. Continuous Integration/Continuous Deployment (CI/CD) pipelines can be set up using tools like Jenkins, GitHub Actions, or cloud provider-specific services. These tools automate the steps from pushing code to a repository to deploying the application on the cloud, ensuring that your application is always up-to-date.

Cost management is a critical aspect of cloud deployments. Cloud platforms operate on a pay-as-you-go model, and without proper management, expenses can escalate quickly. Utilize tools provided by cloud platforms for budgeting and monitoring cloud expenditure. Implementing cost-efficient practices, such as optimizing resource usage and selecting appropriate pricing models, will prevent budget overruns.

Performance optimization is another vital area. Cloud platforms offer the ability to scale resources according to demand, but optimization goes beyond scaling. It involves fine-tuning the application and its environment, caching, database optimization, and employing CDN services for global accessibility. Python developers should leverage the scalability and flexibility of cloud platforms to maximize application performance.

Documentation and support are your allies in the cloud deployment journey. Comprehensive documentation is offered by all major cloud providers, covering a vast array of topics from basic setup to advanced configurations. Furthermore, community forums and official support channels can be invaluable resources when encountering challenges.

Before moving your Python application to the cloud, it's prudent to test it thoroughly in a cloud-based staging environment. This mirrors the production environment but isn't accessible to the public, allowing developers to catch and fix errors before they impact users. Utilizing cloud services for automatic scaling, load balancing, and redundancy ensures that the application remains robust and available under varying load conditions.

In conclusion, deploying Python applications on the cloud involves a series of strategic steps, from selecting a cloud provider to optimizing performance. It's a process that demands a good grasp of cloud concepts, familiarity with containerization and serverless computing, and a diligent approach to security, monitoring, and cost management. With the right tools and practices, Python developers can harness the full potential of the cloud, making their applications more scalable, reliable, and accessible.

Serverless Computing with Python

Transitioning from the established utilities of Python in various applications, we now delve into the realm of serverless computing. This emerging paradigm significantly impacts how developers conceive, construct, and manage software solutions. Particularly for Python developers, the shift towards serverless computing opens up a new horizon of scalable, efficient code deployment without the traditional overhead of server management.

At its core, serverless computing refers to a cloud computing execution model wherein the cloud provider dynamically manages the allocation of machine resources. Unlike traditional architectures, serverless computing allows developers to run their applications without concerning themselves with the infrastructure usually needed to launch and sustain an application. This model can be particularly beneficial for Python developers looking to focus purely on their coding without delving into the intricacies of server configuration and maintenance.

Python's compatibility with serverless architecture stems from its versatile nature and widespread support by major cloud service providers. Popular platforms like AWS Lambda, Google Cloud Functions, and Azure Functions all offer first-class support for Python, enabling developers to deploy a wide variety of applications ranging from simple scripts to complex data processing workflows.

The advantage of serverless computing with Python is multifaceted. Firstly, it abstracts server management, which lowers the barrier to entry for developing and deploying applications. Developers can quickly iterate on their code, pushing updates without concerning themselves with the underlying hardware. Secondly, it offers an economic benefit through a pay-as-you-go pricing model, which aligns closely with the economic constraints of startups and enterprises alike.

Getting started with serverless Python involves understanding the basics of creating, deploying, and managing functions within a serverless environment. A function in this context is a piece of Python code executed in response to certain triggers, such as an HTTP request or a change in a database. Developers will find that most cloud platforms provide CLI tools and SDKs to streamline these tasks.

One of the critical considerations when developing for a serverless environment is state management. Since serverless functions are stateless, any persistent state needs to be stored externally, typically in a database or a cloud storage service. Developers must design their applications in a way that accommodates this constraint, ensuring smooth operation under the serverless model.

Another aspect worth noting is the cold start phenomenon, where the initial invocation of a serverless function may take longer to execute due to the time taken to allocate resources. This can be mitigated through various strategies, such as keeping the functions warm via regular invocations or optimizing the function's dependencies and startup time.

Python's rich ecosystem of libraries and frameworks significantly enhances the serverless experience. Various frameworks, such as Zappa, Chalice, and Serverless Framework, offer tools tailored for deploying Python applications in a serverless setting. These frameworks abstract many of the complexities involved, providing a smoother workflow for Python developers.

Security in serverless Python applications is another critical area. While the cloud provider assumes responsibility for securing the infrastructure, application-level security remains in the developer's hands. Best practices include adopting the principle of least privilege for function permissions, input validation to prevent injection attacks, and encryption for sensitive data both in transit and at rest.

Monitoring and debugging serverless applications present unique challenges. Since developers do not have direct access to the underlying servers, they must rely on the logging and monitoring tools provided by the cloud service provider. Fortunately, these tools have matured significantly, offering deep insights into the application's performance and issues.

Serverless architecture also promotes a microservices design pattern, encouraging the development of small, independently deployable functions that can be developed, maintained, and scaled independently. This can lead to more resilient applications but requires a shift in thinking about application design and inter-service communication.

For developers interested in event-driven programming, serverless computing with Python is a perfect fit. The serverless model inherently supports event-driven architectures, allowing functions to be invoked in response to a wide range of events. This makes it an excellent choice for applications that need to respond in real-time to changes in data, user inputs, or external signals.

In conclusion, serverless computing with Python represents a powerful, flexible approach to building and deploying applications. It offers Python developers the ability to focus on their code, not the underlying infrastructure, while benefiting from the scalability, reliability, and cost-effectiveness of modern cloud platforms. As this technology continues to evolve, it's an area ripe for exploration and innovation within the Python community.

As we transition into the following sections of this book, it's worth pondering how the concepts and practices outlined in this segment can inform and enhance your work, whether you're building web applications, analyzing data, or automating processes with Python. The journey through Python and the cloud is just beginning, and serverless computing is a critical piece of this evolving landscape.

Chapter 18: GUI Programming with Python

Transitioning now to GUI Programming with Python, this chapter unfolds a crucial aspect of developing desktop applications that are both functional and engaging for users. Python, with its vast ecosystem, offers several libraries for crafting graphical user interfaces (GUI), making it accessible for programmers at all levels to create visually appealing applications. In this chapter, we'll embark on exploring Tkinter, Python's standard library for creating GUIs that provides a fast and straightforward way of building simple applications. We'll also delve into PyQt and PySide, which are powerful tools for constructing more sophisticated GUIs with advanced functionalities. These libraries offer extensive customization options, allowing developers to create polished, modern interfaces.

Moreover, for those aiming to develop applications that run seamlessly across different operating systems, Kivy will be introduced as an option for cross-platform development. Kivy emphasizes on multitouch applications but is versatile enough to handle various types of GUI applications. This chapter is structured to guide you through the essential concepts, practical examples, and best practices in GUI programming with Python. Whether you aim to develop simple tools to enhance your productivity, or complex, feature-rich applications, mastering GUI programming significantly expands the horizontals of projects you can undertake. The focus will be on creating interactive interfaces that are user-friendly, efficient, and aesthetically pleasing, leveraging Python's capabilities to enhance user experience.

Tkinter for Desktop Applications

Embarking on the adventure of developing desktop applications with Python, Tkinter emerges as a foundational framework that merits attention. A versatile toolkit, Tkinter provides a robust bridge between Python and Tcl/Tk, enabling the creation of rich graphical user interfaces (GUIs). Given its inclusion with Python's standard library, Tkinter doesn't require separate installation, making it an accessible option for both beginners and seasoned developers alike.

Tkinter operates on the principles of simplicity and effectiveness. By leveraging Tkinter, developers can efficiently prototype and deploy desktop applications that run seamlessly across Windows, macOS, and Linux. This cross-platform compatibility ensures that applications developed with Tkinter can reach a wide audience, irrespective of the operating system.

The structure of a Tkinter application revolves around the creation of a window, also known as the root widget, which serves as the container for all other GUI elements. These elements, ranging from buttons and labels to text fields and canvases, are referred to as widgets in the Tkinter framework. By understanding the hierarchical nature of these widgets and mastering the way they interact, developers can craft intuitive and visually appealing interfaces.

One of the first steps in working with Tkinter is the initialization of the root window. This window acts as the canvas upon which various widgets are drawn. The process is straightforward, demonstrating Tkinter's ease of use and its focus on getting developers up and running with minimal setup.

Widgets in Tkinter are incredibly versatile, each serving a specific function. Buttons, for instance, are used to execute a command upon being clicked, while labels display text or images. Entry widgets allow for text input, making them ideal for forms. Understanding the unique properties and methods of each widget is key to utilizing Tkinter's full potential.

Layout management in Tkinter is another critical area of focus. Tkinter provides three geometry managers - pack, grid, and place - each offering a different approach to widget positioning. The pack manager organizes widgets in blocks, the grid manager arranges them in a table-like structure, and the place manager allows for precise positioning by specifying coordinates. Mastering these managers is essential for creating organized and aesthetically pleasing GUIs.

Event handling in Tkinter allows developers to imbue their applications with interactivity. Through binding functions to widget events, such as button clicks or keyboard presses, applications can respond dynamically to user actions. This capability is crucial for creating engaging and responsive user experiences.

Moreover, Tkinter supports the customization of widget appearance through styling options. Colors, fonts, and sizes can be modified to conform to specific aesthetic or branding requirements, thereby enhancing the visual appeal of applications.

An invaluable feature of Tkinter is its ability to embed other frameworks and technologies. This means developers aren't limited to the capabilities of Tkinter alone; they can incorporate elements like Matplotlib plots or integrate web technologies into their applications for enhanced functionality.

Despite its strengths, it's important for developers to recognize the limitations of Tkinter. For applications requiring advanced graphics or modern UI elements, alternative frameworks like PyQt or PySide might be more appropriate. However, for many standard desktop applications, Tkinter offers a balance of simplicity and functionality that is hard to beat.

Tkinter's documentation and vibrant community provide ample resources for overcoming challenges and learning advanced techniques. Numerous online forums, tutorials, and example projects exist to help developers hone their skills and explore new possibilities with Tkinter.

Real-world applications of Tkinter are diverse, ranging from simple utility tools to more complex business applications. It has been used to develop educational software, productivity tools, and even games, showcasing its versatility.

In conclusion, Tkinter offers an accessible entry point into GUI programming with Python, balancing simplicity with a powerful set of features. Its standard inclusion with Python, cross-platform capabilities, and robust community support make it an excellent choice for desktop application development. By mastering Tkinter, developers can not only enhance their Python programming skills but also unlock new opportunities to create impactful software.

As we delve deeper into the world of GUI programming, it's clear that Tkinter, with its rich capabilities and wide applicability, serves as a solid foundation for developers embarking on this journey. The blend of theory with practical application that Tkinter encourages is key to becoming proficient in developing desktop applications with Python.

Towards the end of this section, it's encouraged for readers to experiment with Tkinter by embarking on small projects. Challenges such as creating a calculator, a basic text editor, or a simple drawing application can significantly aid in solidifying one's understanding of Tkinter and GUI programming principles in Python. With practice and exploration, the path to mastering Tkinter and creating compelling desktop applications is well within reach for Python programmers at any level of expertise.

PyQt/PySide for Advanced GUIs

PyQt and PySide represent two of the most powerful libraries for creating graphical user interfaces (GUIs) in the Python landscape. Both serve as Python bindings for the Qt application framework, a widely used cross-platform framework that enables developers to create applications that can run on various operating systems such as Windows, macOS, and Linux with minimal or no change in the underlying codebase. PyQt is developed by the Riverbank Computing, while PySide is provided by The Qt Company. The core functionalities of both libraries are almost identical, yet they differ in terms of licensing and some minor aspects.

Diving into PyQt or PySide requires an understanding of their object-oriented approach. This is a significant shift from simpler scripting or procedural programming Python developers might be accustomed to. The concept revolves around designing your app as a collection of objects that interact with each other in a cohesive application. This shift not only makes your application more modular and easier to maintain but also leverages the power of Qt's rich set of features for creating professional and sophisticated user interfaces.

The first step to mastering PyQt or PySide is understanding the signal and slot mechanism that Qt uses for event handling. Signals and slots make it easy to create responsive GUIs. In this context, a signal is emitted by an object when its state changes, and a slot is a function that is called in response to the signal. This mechanism decouples the components of the application, making it easier to manage complexity.

One of the strengths of PyQt and PySide is their comprehensive set of widgets that are available out of the box. Widgets are the basic building blocks of a GUI application. These include simple elements such as buttons, labels, and text fields, as well as more complex components like calendars, sliders, and tables. The extensive widget collection enables developers to create complex and feature-rich applications without needing to reinvent the wheel.

Layout management in PyQt and PySide is another critical aspect that developers need to grasp. Unlike some GUI frameworks where positioning of elements is done absolutely, Qt promotes the use of layouts to manage the positioning and sizing of widgets. Layouts make it easier to create interfaces that are flexible and adapt well to different window sizes, resolutions, and user preferences.

Styling and theming are also integral parts of creating applications with PyQt and PySide. Qt uses a CSS-like styling language that allows for detailed customization of widgets and controls. This means that beyond the functionality, developers can also ensure that the applications match the branding or aesthetic requirements of the project or organization. The ability to theme applications similarly helps in maintaining a consistent look and feel across platforms.

For developers looking to create data-driven applications, integrating with model-view programming frameworks is essential. PyQt and PySide both support a model-view-controller (MVC) like architecture with their model-view classes. This design pattern separates the data (model) from the user interface (view) and the application logic (controller), making the codebase easier to manage and scale.

Another compelling feature of PyQt and PySide is the support for creating custom widgets. While the standard set of widgets is extensive, there might be scenarios where a specific functionality or visualization is required that is not available out of the box. In such cases, developers have the ability to extend existing widgets or create entirely new ones that seamlessly integrate with the app's existing components.

Internationalization and localization are critical for applications that aim for a global audience. PyQt and PySide provide tools and mechanisms to translate your application into multiple languages without significant changes to the codebase. This feature ensures that developers can create applications that are accessible to users worldwide, thereby increasing the potential user base.

For those concerned with application performance, PyQt and PySide offer several mechanisms to ensure applications run smoothly and efficiently. They include support for threading and multiprocessing to handle long-running operations or tasks that can potentially block the user interface. This ensures the applications remain responsive, providing a better user experience.

Testing and debugging are vital components of any software development process, and GUI applications are no exception. PyQt and PySide are compatible with Python's standard testing frameworks, allowing developers to automate testing of their applications' user interfaces. This ensures that applications are robust and reliable before release.

Deployment of PyQt and PySide applications is facilitated by the array of packaging tools available in the Python ecosystem. Tools such as PyInstaller and cx_Freeze can bundle PyQt or PySide applications along with the Python interpreter and all necessary dependencies into a standalone executable that can be distributed and run on target systems without requiring Python to be installed.

Learning PyQt or PySide can be daunting given their complexity and the range of concepts that developers must familiarize themselves with. However, the investment in mastering these libraries is justified by the level of professionalism and sophistication they bring to Python GUI applications. With an active community and a wealth of documentation and tutorials, getting started and advancing in PyQt or PySide is more accessible than ever.

In conclusion, PyQt and PySide offer an array of features for advanced GUI development in Python. By understanding the foundational concepts such as signal-slot mechanism, widget usage, layout management, and leveraging the advanced features like custom widget creation, internationalization, and application packaging, developers can create professional, efficient, and user-friendly desktop applications. The journey from beginner to proficient in PyQt or PySide GUI development is a challenging yet rewarding path that opens the door to creating powerful desktop applications with Python.

Cross-Platform Development with Kivy

Building applications that run smoothly across different platforms is a common challenge faced by developers today. Python, known for its versatility and simplicity, offers an effective solution to this problem through Kivy - a free and open-source Python library. Kivy is specifically designed for the rapid development of applications that benefit from innovative user interfaces, such as multi-touch apps.

Kivy stands out in the realm of GUI programming with its ability to run on Android, iOS, Linux, OS X, and Windows. This cross-platform nature ensures that developers can create an application once and deploy it across multiple platforms with minimal adjustments. This is particularly appealing for those looking to maximize the reach of their software with reduced development times and costs.

At its core, Kivy operates on a novel event-driven framework that leverages the native inputs, protocols, and devices of each platform. This approach allows for the design of rich, engaging interfaces that are responsive and intuitive to use. The framework's modular architecture also means that you can use only the components you need, keeping your application lightweight and optimized.

One of the key advantages of Kivy for beginners and experienced developers alike is its extensive documentation and active community.

The Kivy website provides tutorials, examples, and a comprehensive guide to help you get started with the framework. Whether you're looking to create games, business applications, or anything in between, you'll find resources to support your development journey.

Kivy's graphical engine, built over OpenGL ES 2, uses a modern and fast graphics pipeline. For developers, this translates into the ability to craft fluid multi-touch experiences that are visually stunning without needing to dive deep into the complexities of OpenGL programming.

The language used for creating layouts and widgets in Kivy is called the Kv language. This custom-designed language facilitates rapid UI development and encourages a clean separation between logic and presentation in your applications. By defining your UI and its interactions in a declarative manner, you can achieve a higher level of maintainability and scalability in your projects.

Furthermore, Kivy comes with a wide array of built-in widgets, from basic buttons and text inputs to more complex elements like carousels and accordions. These widgets are highly customizable and can be extended or modified to fit the specific needs of your application. For developers, this means more time can be spent on implementing unique features rather than reinventing the wheel.

Kivy also excels in its deployment capabilities. With tools like Buildozer and Pyjnius for Android or Pyobjus for iOS, compiling your app into a package that's ready to distribute on app stores or distribute to other users is straightforward. This process simplifies the often complex task of deploying to multiple platforms, making your development workflow much smoother.

Despite its many benefits, Kivy does come with a learning curve. Understanding how to effectively leverage the Kv language and navigate Kivy's event-driven system can take time. However, the investment in learning this framework pays dividends in the long run, through significantly reduced development times and the ability to deliver applications to a wider audience.

Given the rise of mobile apps and the constant demand for cross-platform solutions, Kivy's relevance in the current tech landscape cannot be overstated. For Python developers, it represents a powerful tool in the arsenal for tackling modern software challenges. Whether you are a hobbyist looking to bring your ideas to life or a professional developing enterprise-level applications, Kivy offers the capabilities to turn your visions into reality.

In this section, we have explored the essential aspects of cross-platform development with Kivy. From its design philosophy and core features to the practical benefits it offers, Kivy emerges as a formidable choice for GUI programming in Python. As with any technology, the best way to understand what Kivy is capable of is to start working with it. Experimenting with the framework and building small projects can be an enlightening experience, offering insights into efficient cross-platform development practices.

To those venturing into the world of GUI programming with Python, exploring Kivy presents an opportunity to not only learn a highly efficient framework but also to engage with a vibrant community of developers. The challenges you face along the way will not only enhance your understanding of graphical application development but also improve your ability to think in terms of multi-platform solutions. Embarking on this journey can be the key to unlocking a new level of creativity and innovation in your Python projects.

In conclusion, Kivy embodies the spirit of Python programming - powerful, versatile, and accessible. As we continue to advance in a digital age where the boundaries between platforms are increasingly blurred, tools like Kivy that foster innovation and inclusivity are more important than ever. It's an exciting time to be a Python developer, and Kivy is just one of the many tools that make this journey so rewarding.

Chapter 19:
Python and the Internet of Things (IoT)

In the realm of the Internet of Things (IoT), Python has emerged as a significant enabler, powering a plethora of devices and applications that interconnect our physical world with the digital realm. This chapter delves into how Python's versatility and ease of use make it an ideal programming language for developing IoT projects. Beginning with an exploration of Python's role in the burgeoning IoT landscape, it specifically highlights how Python's simplicity allows for rapid prototyping while its robustness enables the deployment of reliable IoT systems. A closer look is taken at the utilization of Python on the Raspberry Pi, a popular platform for DIY IoT projects due to its affordability and powerful capabilities. The discussion then shifts to IoT protocols such as MQTT and CoAP, detailing how Python supports these protocols to facilitate efficient communication between IoT devices. Furthermore, readers are guided through a selection of real-world Python IoT projects, providing tangible insights into how Python is applied in practical scenarios to solve real-world challenges. Through this exploration, the chapter aims to equip readers with the knowledge and skills to harness Python's potential in crafting innovative IoT solutions that bridge the gap between the physical and digital worlds, thereby expanding the horizons of what's possible with Python.

Python on the Raspberry Pi

The Raspberry Pi, a small, affordable, and versatile computer, has become an essential tool in the world of Internet of Things (IoT). It is particularly favored among hobbyists, educators, and developers alike for its ease of use and flexibility. One of the key reasons for its popularity in these circles is its support for Python, making it an accessible platform for a wide range of projects, from simple beginner experiments to sophisticated professional applications.

Python's readability and concise syntax make it an ideal first programming language for those new to the Raspberry Pi. The Python ecosystem, with its vast array of libraries and frameworks, further extends the capabilities of the Raspberry Pi, allowing users to interact with various sensors and hardware, develop user interfaces, and communicate over the Internet.

One of the most significant advantages of using Python on the Raspberry Pi is the GPIO (General Purpose Input Output) library. This Python module simplifies the process of writing scripts to control pins, read sensors, and interface with other devices, directly from the Pi. It's an invaluable tool for creating interactive hardware projects without needing an extensive background in electronics.

Threading and multiprocessing in Python also play critical roles when working on more demanding applications on the Raspberry Pi. These features allow for the development of efficient programs that can perform multiple tasks simultaneously, a necessity in many IoT projects that require real-time data processing and analysis.

Moreover, various Python IDEs (Integrated Development Environments) and code editors are available that run smoothly on the Raspberry Pi. These tools provide autocompletion, syntax highlighting, and debugging features that significantly enhance the coding experience. They cater to developers of all skill levels, helping beginners to learn and professionals to speed up their workflow.

Networking is another area where Python on the Raspberry Pi shines. With libraries such as socket programming, developers can easily implement client-server applications. This capability is particularly useful in IoT projects that involve remote monitoring and control of devices over the Internet.

For those interested in web development, Python's Flask and Django frameworks are also compatible with the Raspberry Pi. These tools allow developers to design and deploy web applications directly from their Pi, turning it into a low-cost, energy-efficient server.

The Raspberry Pi's camera module, coupled with Python's OpenCV library, opens up a whole new world of possibilities for creative projects. From building a time-lapse rig to developing a motion-sensing security camera, Python makes it straightforward to capture and process images and video.

Data storage and retrieval are crucial aspects of many IoT projects. Python's support for various database systems, including SQLite, MongoDB, and even cloud-based solutions, means that Raspberry Pi users can easily store, access, and manage large volumes of data.

Python's role in machine learning and artificial intelligence also extends to the Raspberry Pi. Libraries like TensorFlow and Scikit-learn are available for the platform, enabling the development of projects that require pattern recognition, natural language processing, and other AI functionalities.

The growing community of Python developers and the wealth of online resources and tutorials specifically targeted at Raspberry Pi users further enrich the learning experience. From forums and blogs to video tutorials, there's an abundance of support available for those embarking on their Python and Raspberry Pi journey.

Education is another area where Python on the Raspberry Pi has made a significant impact. Its affordability and the interactive nature of hardware projects make it an engaging tool for teaching programming and computer science concepts. Schools around the world have adopted the Raspberry Pi as a means of introducing students to coding, electronics, and data analysis.

The versatility of Python on the Raspberry Pi also means that it can be used for professional application development and prototyping. Businesses are using Pi-based solutions for everything from digital signage and point-of-sale systems to sophisticated monitoring and control systems in manufacturing and agriculture.

In conclusion, Python's integration with the Raspberry Pi has played a pivotal role in the growth of the IoT. It has democratized access to programming and electronics, making it possible for anyone with an idea to bring it to life. Whether you're a beginner looking to learn the basics of coding or an experienced developer working on cutting-edge projects, the combination of Python and the Raspberry Pi offers an expansive playground for exploration and innovation.

The future of Python on the Raspberry Pi looks promising, with continuous updates to both the hardware and software. As the Raspberry Pi becomes more powerful and Python's libraries grow even more comprehensive, the possibilities for new and exciting projects are limitless. It's an exciting time to dive into the world of Python and IoT with the Raspberry Pi at your side.

IoT Protocols and Python

In the burgeoning landscape of the Internet of Things (IoT), where devices ranging from home thermostats to industrial machines are becoming interconnected, the importance of effective communication protocols can't be overstated. Python, with its simplicity and versatility, emerges as a quintessential tool in the development and implementation of these protocols. This section delves into how Python facilitates the use of various IoT protocols, empowering developers to craft solutions that are both robust and scalable.

At the heart of IoT systems lie various protocols, each designed to cater to specific requirements pertaining to efficiency, reliability, and security. Protocols such as MQTT (Message Queuing Telemetry Transport), CoAP (Constrained Application Protocol), and HTTP/HTTPS are foundational to IoT ecosystems, enabling devices to communicate seamlessly despite the constraints of power or bandwidth.

MQTT, a lightweight messaging protocol, is particularly favored in IoT for its efficient bandwidth usage and its ability to facilitate bidirectional communication between devices. Python libraries like **paho-mqtt** provide a straightforward interface for connecting, publishing, and subscribing to MQTT brokers, thereby simplifying the process of integrating MQTT into IoT solutions.

Similarly, CoAP, designed for simple electronic devices, allows for effective operation in constrained environments, making it a go-to choice for many IoT applications. The **aiocoap** library, for instance, leverages Python's asynchronous features to offer a comprehensive toolkit for CoAP communication, thereby harnessing Python's capability to manage asynchronous I/O operations for enhanced scalability.

Moreover, while HTTP/HTTPS may not be as lightweight as MQTT or CoAP, it remains a relevant protocol, especially for IoT devices that require secure, restful interactions. Python's **requests** and **flask** libraries are instrumental in integrating HTTP/HTTPS communication in IoT systems, demonstrating Python's flexibility in adapting to diverse protocol requirements.

Understanding the nuances of these protocols and their implementation in Python requires a grasp of the underlying principles of IoT connectivity. Devices in an IoT network must efficiently manage power and bandwidth while ensuring timely and reliable communication. The choice of protocol, therefore, hinges on the specific application's demands, be it low power consumption, real-time updates, or secure transmissions.

The role of Python extends beyond merely offering libraries for protocol implementation. It also fosters a community where developers can share insights, tools, and libraries, further accelerating IoT development. Community-contributed modules and frameworks encapsulate best practices and innovative solutions, enabling even novice developers to build sophisticated IoT applications.

Another significant advantage of using Python for IoT protocols is its cross-platform nature, ensuring that code written for one type of device can be easily ported to another with minimal modifications. Such flexibility is invaluable in the IoT domain, where devices often run on various operating systems and hardware configurations.

Security in IoT communication is paramount, as devices frequently transmit sensitive data. Python's support for encryption libraries, such as **pycryptodome**, helps in securing device communications adhering to protocols like MQTT over SSL/TLS, safeguarding data against potential breaches.

Efficient data serialization and deserialization are critical for IoT devices to interpret and exchange data correctly. Python libraries like **json** and **protobuf** are extensively used in IoT applications for this purpose, again underscoring Python's utility in handling protocol-specific data formats.

Furthermore, testing and debugging IoT applications are made more accessible by Python's rich ecosystem of development tools.

Libraries such as **pytest** and **pdb** allow for rigorous testing of protocol implementations, ensuring reliability and robustness in IoT applications.

In the development of IoT systems that require interaction with web services or APIs, Python's simplicity in handling HTTP requests and processing JSON data shines, allowing devices to seamlessly integrate with the broader internet ecosystem. This capability is crucial for scenarios where IoT devices rely on external services for functionalities such as weather data, geolocation, and more.

While leveraging Python for IoT, one must also consider the constraints of the devices involved. Although Python is inherently resource-efficient, further optimizations may be necessary for devices with limited processing power or memory. Techniques such as using lighter libraries or compiling Python code to C using tools like Cython can help in deploying Python applications on constrained devices without compromising performance.

As IoT continues to evolve, new protocols and standards will emerge to address emerging challenges and opportunities. Python's adaptability and extensive library ecosystem position it as an enduring tool for IoT developers, enabling them to navigate the evolving landscape with confidence and creativity.

In conclusion, the synergy between IoT protocols and Python represents a powerful paradigm for the development of interconnected devices and systems. Python's simplicity, combined with its powerful libraries and supportive community, offers an unparalleled toolkit for implementing and innovating within the IoT space. As developers continue to push the boundaries of what's possible in IoT, Python's role in this domain is set to expand, offering promising avenues for exploration and application.

Real-World Python IoT Projects

Entering the realm of real-world Python projects for the Internet of Things (IoT) presents a fascinating blend of challenges and opportunities. IoT, a system of interrelated computing devices with the ability to transfer data over a network without requiring human-to-computer interaction, has seen tremendous growth. Python, with its simplicity and robust ecosystem, has become a favored language for IoT development. This section delves into practical Python IoT projects, highlighting the versatility and power of Python in solving real-world problems.

An initial project that beginners might find engaging involves constructing a home temperature monitoring system using a Raspberry Pi. Equipped with a temperature sensor, the Raspberry Pi can collect temperature data and use Python scripts to process this information. Users can then view the data through a simple web interface or receive alerts when temperatures reach certain thresholds. This project not only introduces hardware interaction but also covers data collection, processing, and web development basics with Python.

Moving beyond basic data collection, another intriguing project is the creation of a smart irrigation system. By integrating soil moisture sensors with actuators like water pumps, Python can be used to automate watering in gardens or farms. This project can expand to involve weather forecast data fetching using Python to optimize watering schedules, thereby conserving water and ensuring optimal plant growth.

For those interested in wearable technology, developing a step counter using Python offers a hands-on experience. By utilizing an accelerometer connected to a microcontroller that can run Python, like the MicroPython board, developers can create algorithms to detect steps and track daily activity. This project can further evolve into designing a complete fitness tracker, showcasing Python's capability to handle data from various sensors and manage complex calculations.

Home automation projects offer another arena to apply Python in IoT. Imagine a system that controls lights, temperature, and even plays music based on voice commands or preset conditions. Python's libraries can interface with hardware to turn on/off devices, and frameworks like Flask can be used to create a web or mobile app as a control panel. This integration demonstrates Python's role in creating smart environments.

On a more advanced level, Python can drive the development of a security monitoring system. By connecting cameras and motion detectors, Python scripts can analyze video feeds in real time to detect unusual activities. Utilizing libraries like OpenCV for image processing and TensorFlow for machine learning, the system can identify people, pets, and other objects, sending alerts or triggering alarms based on specific criteria.

Environmental monitoring projects also showcase Python's adaptability in IoT. Sensors measuring air quality, humidity, or radiation can feed data into a Python-powered system that models environmental conditions over time. Such projects not only contribute to scientific research but also raise awareness of environmental issues within communities.

For urban development, Python's application in smart traffic management systems illustrates its potential to address modern challenges. By analyzing traffic flow data in real-time from cameras and sensors on roads, Python algorithms can optimize traffic lights sequences, reducing congestion and improving urban mobility.

In healthcare, patient monitoring systems based on IoT devices can collect vital signs and use Python for data analysis and real-time alerting to healthcare professionals. This involves complex data processing and integration with medical databases, reflecting Python's capacity for handling sensitive and critical information.

Python's versatility extends to agricultural projects as well. Smart farming techniques, such as using drones for crop analysis, soil moisture sensors for intelligent watering, and automated harvesters, rely on Python for task automation and data analysis, demonstrating the language's ability to tackle diverse and scalable projects.

The burgeoning field of smart manufacturing also benefits from Python's proficiency. Factories equipped with sensors on machinery can use Python for predictive maintenance, analyzing data patterns to forecast potential breakdowns before they occur, optimizing productivity and reducing downtimes.

Engaging in Python IoT projects necessitates a foundation in Python programming, an understanding of hardware components, and the ability to integrate software with hardware. Projects range from simple temperature sensors to complex systems like smart traffic lights or patient monitoring, each offering unique challenges and learning opportunities.

Successfully executing these projects requires diving into Python's libraries and frameworks, understanding IoT protocols, and often, collaborative development techniques. While some projects might start off as a hobby or a learning exercise, they have the potential to scale into solutions that address real-world problems, benefitting society at large.

The journey through real-world Python IoT projects not only enhances coding skills but also fosters an inventive mindset, preparing individuals to create impactful technologies. As the IoT landscape evolves, Python programmers are well-positioned to lead innovations, transforming the interconnected world with every line of code.

In conclusion, the intersection of Python and IoT opens up a world of possibilities for creating intelligent systems that improve lives and conserve resources. From home automation to environmental monitoring, healthcare, and beyond, Python stands as a pillar in the development of IoT solutions, inspiring a new age of inventors and problem solvers.

Chapter 20: Collaborative Development with Python

In this pivotal chapter, we delve into the essential practices and tools that enable Python programmers to collaborate effectively on projects. Collaboration in software development not only accelerates the coding process but also significantly improves the quality of the code through diverse perspectives and expertise. One of the foundational tools in this domain is Git, a version control system, alongside GitHub, a platform for hosting Git repositories online, facilitating code sharing and collaboration. We will guide you through setting up and using these tools, ensuring smooth collaborative workflows. Moreover, the importance of virtual environments cannot be overstated; they are crucial for managing project-specific dependencies without conflicting with the global Python installation or other projects. This chapter also emphasizes the value of code reviews and pair programming, practices that foster learning, enhance coding skills, and ensure code quality. Through code reviews, developers can provide constructive feedback on each other's code, leading to better solutions and personal growth. Pair programming, on the other hand, involves two programmers working together at one workstation, effectively combining their expertise to solve problems more efficiently. By mastering these collaborative tools and practices, you'll be well-equipped to contribute to Python projects in any professional environment, leveraging the collective intelligence of your team to achieve exceptional results.

Using Git and GitHub

In the journey of learning and applying Python in various domains, collaboration emerges as a pivotal factor in the development process. The ability to work together on projects, share code, and track changes are foundational to successful software development. Git and GitHub stand out as essential tools for collaborative development, offering a robust platform for version control and code sharing. This section delves into the basics of using Git and GitHub, tailored for Python programmers at any skill level.

Git is a distributed version control system that allows individual developers and teams to track changes in source code during software development. It facilitates the management of modifications and supports collaboration by allowing multiple contributors to merge changes into a single project. GitHub, on the other hand, is a cloud-based hosting service that leverages Git's version control capabilities. It provides a web-based interface to manage Git repositories, fostering collaboration among development teams.

To begin with Git, one must first understand its core concept: the repository. A repository (or repo) contains all of the project's files and stores the history of changes. Developers clone a repository to make a local copy on their computer, where they can work independently, commit changes, and push updates back to the remote repository hosted on GitHub or another service.

Setting up Git involves installing the software on your local machine and configuring basic settings like your name and email address. This personal information is attached to your commits, which are snapshots of your repository at a given point in time. Commit messages, which accompany each commit, offer a description of the changes made, providing context for other contributors.

The first step in using GitHub is creating an account on the platform. Once logged in, you can create new repositories, manage existing ones, and contribute to other projects. GitHub's interface allows you to perform many Git operations without needing to use the command line, though mastering both interfaces is beneficial.

Branching is a core feature of Git that enables divergent development from the main code base, typically used for developing new features or testing. Each branch represents an independent line of development. Once the work on a branch is complete and tested, it can be merged back into the main branch, often called 'master' or 'main'.

Collaboration in Git revolves around the pull request model on GitHub. Developers fork a repository, make changes in a new branch, and then submit a pull request. This process signals to the original repository's maintainers that there's new code to review, discuss, and possibly merge.

Conflicts may arise when merging branches, especially if multiple people modify the same lines of code or if one branch incorporates a significant amount of changes while another is still in development. Git provides tools to resolve these conflicts, allowing users to manually choose which changes to keep.

To maintain code quality and ensure that every addition aligns with the project's direction, GitHub offers features like code reviews. Code reviews allow other developers to examine changes before they are merged, providing feedback and suggesting improvements. This practice not only improves code quality but also fosters learning and mentorship within a team.

GitHub's integration with various Continuous Integration (CI) and Continuous Deployment (CD) tools automates the process of testing code and deploying it to production environments. These integrations can run automated tests every time a new commit is made to a repository, ensuring that new code does not introduce bugs.

For developers using Python, managing project dependencies is streamlined with GitHub. By including a 'requirements.txt' file in a repository, you can list all the required libraries for your project, allowing others to easily replicate your development environment. This practice is crucial for collaborative Python projects to ensure compatibility across different development setups.

Open-source projects benefit greatly from using GitHub, as it provides a centralized platform for managing contributions from anyone in the community. Python developers find GitHub an invaluable resource for hosting their projects, contributing to other open-source initiatives, and showcasing their work to potential employers or collaborators.

Security is another aspect where GitHub aids developers. With features like security alerts, GitHub can automatically scan your project's dependencies for known vulnerabilities and suggest fixes or updates. This proactive approach helps maintain the security integrity of your Python projects.

In conclusion, mastering Git and GitHub is essential for Python developers looking to engage in collaborative development. The ability to track changes, collaborate with others, and manage project dependencies elevates the development process, ensuring that teams can work more efficiently and effectively. As the landscape of software development evolves, these tools remain at the forefront of enabling innovation and collaboration.

Whether you're a beginner or an advanced Python programmer, incorporating these practices into your development workflow will not only enhance your coding skills but also prepare you for professional collaboration in any programming endeavor. The knowledge of Git and GitHub transcends individual projects, offering a foundation for contributing to the broader Python community and beyond.

Virtual Environments and Dependency Management

In the realm of Python development, collaboration is often the key to success. Whether you're working on large-scale applications, academic research, or personal projects, the ability to work effectively with others can greatly enhance both the quality and efficiency of your work. A cornerstone of this collaborative effort is understanding and utilizing virtual environments and dependency management. These tools are critical for isolating project-specific dependencies and ensuring that all team members are working within consistent, controlled development environments.

Virtual environments are, at their core, a self-contained directory tree that includes a Python installation for a particular version of Python, along with a number of additional packages. When activated, the virtual environment's Python interpreter is used as the default "python", and any Python packages installed while the environment is activated are isolated from the system-wide Python installation. This prevents different projects, which may require different versions of the same package, from interfering with each other.

Dependency management, on the other hand, involves identifying, installing, and managing the packages your project requires. Dependencies can include libraries, frameworks, or other resources your code needs to function correctly. Proper dependency management ensures that all necessary packages are installed, at the correct versions, for anyone who works with your code. This is crucial for avoiding the infamous "It works on my machine" syndrome, where code runs perfectly on one developer's setup but fails in another's due to missing or mismatching dependencies.

The combination of virtual environments and dependency management tools like pip and virtualenv facilitates a robust workflow for Python projects. Pip, the Python package installer, allows developers to install, upgrade, and remove packages. Virtualenv, meanwhile, is the tool that creates isolated Python environments. Together, they enable developers to manage dependencies efficiently, avoiding conflicts between projects and making it easier to collaborate with others.

To begin leveraging these tools, one must first understand how to create a virtual environment. Using virtualenv, a developer can create an environment with a simple command line instruction. Once activated, any Python or pip commands will operate within the scope of the virtual environment, unaffected by system-wide installations. This siloed approach ensures that any actions taken — whether adding, removing, or updating Python packages — will not impact other development work occurring outside the environment.

Furthermore, an integral part of working collaboratively is ensuring that all team members can replicate the project's development environment. This is where requirements files come into play. A requirements file is a list of all of a project's dependencies, including the precise versions of each package. By including this file in a project's repository, any developer can create an identical environment by using pip to install all necessary packages at once. This drastically simplifies the process of setting up one's development environment and ensures consistency across the board.

One must also consider the version control of these requirements files. As projects evolve, dependencies may change. New packages might be added, or existing ones may be upgraded or removed. Regularly updating the requirements file and tracking these changes through version control systems like Git ensures that all collaborators are always in sync with the project's current state. This practice minimizes conflicts arising from outdated environments or incompatible dependencies.

Another aspect worth noting is the role of environment variables. These can be used within virtual environments to further customize and control the behavior of Python applications. By setting environment-specific variables, developers can configure applications to run differently in development, testing, and production environments. This can be essential for safeguarding sensitive data, such as API keys or database credentials, which should not be hard-coded into applications or stored in version control.

It's also important to address potential challenges in virtual environments and dependency management. One such challenge is dealing with transitive dependencies — packages that your project's direct dependencies require. The complexity of managing these indirect dependencies increases with the size and scope of the project. Tools like Pipenv and Poetry offer more sophisticated dependency resolution mechanisms, attempting to solve these complications by creating lock files. These tools ensure that not just the direct dependencies, but also the correct versions of all transitive dependencies, are consistently replicated across environments.

Despite these complexities, the benefits of properly managed virtual environments are manifold. They empower developers to experiment with new packages or versions without risk, facilitate smoother project handoffs, and enhance security by isolating dependencies. Moreover, when combined with containerization technologies such as Docker, virtual environments can become even more powerful. Containers can encapsulate entire runtime environments, including the operating system, Python interpreter, libraries, and code, ensuring even greater consistency and portability across development, testing, and production environments.

In conclusion, mastering virtual environments and dependency management is indispensable for Python developers aiming for effective collaboration. By isolating project dependencies, maintaining consistent development environments, and utilizing tools like pip, virtualenv, Pipenv, and Poetry, developers can mitigate many common challenges in software development. As with any toolset, there is a learning curve, but the investment in understanding and applying these practices pays dividends in the form of more robust, reliable, and collaborative Python projects.

To further explore these concepts and tools, developers are encouraged to experiment with creating their own virtual environments, managing dependencies for different projects, and integrating advanced tools into their workflows. Continuous learning and adaptation are key to staying proficient in these practices, enabling not only individual growth but also fostering healthier and more productive development teams.

Code Reviews and Pair Programming

As we delve deeper into collaborative development with Python, we encounter two crucial practices that significantly boost the quality of code and foster learning among team members: code reviews and pair programming. These methodologies not only improve the codebase but also cultivate a collaborative culture within the development team. In this section, we'll explore these practices in detail, uncovering how they fit into the Python programming environment and contribute to the growth of both individual programmers and the project as a whole.

Code reviews, a standard practice in software development, involve systematically examining code written by a colleague. This process not only identifies bugs and potential improvements but also serves as a platform for knowledge sharing and standardizing coding practices across the team. In the context of Python, code reviews are particularly valuable given the language's emphasis on readability and the Pythonic way of solving problems. They ensure that solutions are not only functional but also align with the idiomatic use of Python, making the code more maintainable and understandable for current and future team members.

When initiating a code review process within a Python project, it's important to approach it with a mindset of mutual respect and constructive feedback. The objective is to enhance the code and the developers' skills, not to critique personal coding styles negatively. Effective code reviews are characterized by clear, actionable feedback that is supportive and aimed at improving overall code quality. Tools such as pull requests on GitHub provide an excellent platform for conducting code reviews, allowing for inline comments, discussions, and suggestions for changes.

Pair programming, on the other hand, is a more interactive and collaborative approach. It involves two developers working together at one workstation to write code. One, the "driver," writes code while the other, the "navigator," reviews each line of code as it's written, providing insights and direction. The roles are periodically switched, allowing both participants to actively engage in coding and reviewing. This technique is particularly effective in Python projects due to the language's simplicity and readability, making it easier for the navigator to follow along and suggest improvements in real time.

The benefits of pair programming extend beyond mere code quality. It serves as an excellent learning tool, allowing less experienced developers to gain insight from their more experienced counterparts. Likewise, it encourages the exchange of ideas and solutions, fostering a deeper understanding of the Python language and its myriad of frameworks and libraries. Pair programming enhances team communication and collaboration, significantly reducing the likelihood of misinterpretation or overlooking critical issues.

Implementing pair programming in a Python project requires some logistical planning, especially in terms of scheduling and pairing dynamics. It's essential to pair developers with complementary skill sets to maximize learning opportunities and productivity. Additionally, the use of collaborative coding tools that support real-time code sharing and editing can facilitate remote pair programming sessions, allowing the practice to thrive in distributed teams.

It's important to note that both code reviews and pair programming should not be seen as panaceas but as part of a broader set of best practices for Python development. They fit into a comprehensive strategy aimed at improving code quality, developer proficiency, and team dynamics. Emphasizing communication and constructive feedback is key to maximizing the benefits of these practices.

Regarding implementing these practices in your Python projects, start small and gradually increase their frequency. Begin with informal code reviews among team members and introduce pair programming sessions for complex feature development or bug fixing. Over time, as the team becomes more comfortable with these practices, they can be made more formal and integrated into the regular development workflow.

It's also beneficial to complement code reviews and pair programming with other Python-specific tools and practices. For instance, leveraging linters and formatters, such as Flake8 and Black, can automate the enforcement of coding standards, allowing developers to focus on more substantive issues during code reviews and pair programming sessions.

In conclusion, code reviews and pair programming are invaluable practices for collaborative Python development. They not only enhance code quality and project maintainability but also foster a culture of learning and collaboration within the team. By embracing these practices, Python developers can not only improve their code but also grow as professionals, contributing to the development of robust, efficient, and high-quality Python applications.

As this chapter progresses, keep in mind that the cornerstone of these practices is not the sheer act of reviewing or pairing but the ongoing communication and feedback loops they create. These practices should not be rigid but rather adapt to the specific needs and dynamics of your team. The ultimate goal is to build a culture where knowledge sharing, continuous improvement, and mutual support are the norms, significantly contributing to the success and vitality of Python projects.

Whether you're a beginner just starting your Python journey, an intermediate developer looking to deepen your understanding, or an advanced programmer aiming to refine your practices, incorporating code reviews, and pair programming into your development process can markedly accelerate your growth and ensure the delivery of high-quality software. So, as you navigate through the vast landscape of Python programming, keep these collaborative practices in mind—they might just be the catalysts you need to elevate your coding skills and projects to new heights.

Chapter 21: Python for Game Development

Transforming ideas into a captivating game requires not only creativity but also the right set of tools and languages that bring those ideas to life. Among these tools, Python has emerged as a formidable option for both beginners and seasoned developers in the realm of game development. Its simplicity combined with powerful libraries like Pygame allows for rapid development and prototyping of games, making the journey from concept to playable product smoother and more efficient. This chapter delves into the essentials of using Python for creating engaging games, highlighting its application in both 2D and 3D gaming environments through popular frameworks and engines compatible with Python. Further, it walks readers through the process of building a simple game from scratch, illustrating key game development concepts along the way. Whether you're looking to create your first game or leverage Python's capabilities for more complex game development projects, this chapter is designed to equip you with the foundational knowledge needed to venture into the exciting world of game development with Python.

Game Development with Pygame

Exploring the realms of game development using Python introduces us to Pygame, a set of Python modules designed for writing video games. Pygame adds functionality on top of the excellent SDL library, allowing for real-time game development in a way that is both approachable and highly customizable. It's a gateway for beginners into the world of game programming, while also offering the depth needed by experienced developers.

Starting with Pygame does not require extensive knowledge of game development or programming. Its architecture is such that newcomers can jump in by learning just a few basic commands and concepts. This simplicity coexists with the power to build complex visual environments, handle user input, and manage aspects of sound, making it a versatile library for game creation.

Installing Pygame is the first step towards building your own games. It's as simple as running **pip install pygame** in your command-line interface (CLI). This simplicity in setup reflects the overall philosophy of Pygame - making game development accessible and less intimidating for newcomers.

The core concept behind Pygame is the *event loop*. Most games built with Pygame run inside an infinite loop, checking for user events, updating game states, and redrawing the screen accordingly. Understanding this cycle is crucial for developing games that respond to user actions in real-time.

Handling user input in Pygame is straightforward. Whether it's keyboard strokes or mouse clicks, Pygame offers intuitive methods for detecting and responding to these actions. This allows developers to create interactive and dynamic gameplay experiences quite easily.

Graphics in Pygame are managed through *Surfaces*, a kind of object that represents either the game window or an image asset within the game. Drawing and rendering these surfaces are fundamental skills in Pygame, allowing for the visualization of the game elements, from backgrounds to characters.

Another important aspect of game development is animation. Pygame facilitates this by enabling the movement of game elements across the screen through changing their positions in each frame of the game loop. When combined with user input, this allows for interactive and engaging gameplay.

Sound effects and music play a crucial role in creating an immersive gaming experience. With Pygame, integrating sound is as simple as dealing with graphics. It supports various formats and allows for easy playback of background music or sound effects upon specific events in the game.

Optimization is a critical concern in game development. Pygame offers various techniques to ensure games run smoothly. This includes managing how often the game state is updated and rendered, as well as efficiently managing memory and resources by reusing game objects.

After mastering these basics, developers can leverage Pygame's capabilities to develop games that are more complex. Pygame is not limited to 2D games; with some creativity and additional libraries, developers can venture into 3D game development as well.

Pygame's community is an invaluable resource. From detailed documentation to a vast array of tutorials and forums, the community support is robust. This is beneficial for troubleshooting, learning best practices, and discovering innovative approaches to game development.

Despite its simplicity, Pygame is used in professional game projects, proving its capability to power games that require a high level of detail and performance. This showcases Pygame's range, from educational tools to professional-grade game development.

Building a game from scratch entails not just understanding programming but also game design principles. Pygame creates a unique opportunity to practice these principles by simplifying the technical aspects, allowing developers to focus on creativity and design.

Pygame continues to evolve, with regular updates that add new features, enhance performance, and extend compatibility. Keeping up with these updates ensures developers can use the latest functionalities, maintaining the relevance and efficiency of their games.

In summary, Pygame represents a blend of simplicity and power in the domain of game development with Python. It paves the way for beginners to embark on their game development journey, while also serving as a tool for experienced developers to bring intricate game ideas to life. As we delve further into Python's applications in game development, Pygame stands out as a pivotal framework that marries the ease of Python with the complexity and enjoyment of game creation.

D and 3D Game Engines Compatible with Python

Python offers an extensive selection of tools and libraries for game development, which includes several powerful engines compatible with both 2D and 3D game creation. These engines not only streamline the development process but also open up a realm of possibilities for developers, ranging from beginners to those with advanced programming skills. Understanding these engines' capabilities and how they integrate with Python can greatly enhance your game development projects.

One of the most renowned engines in the Python ecosystem is Pygame. Primarily focused on 2D game development, Pygame provides a set of Python modules designed for writing video games. It allows for the creation of games that are both simple and complex, offering control over elements like sound, graphics, and input devices. Despite its focus on 2D, creative developers can also craft simple 3D games using this engine, showcasing its flexibility.

For those looking to delve into more advanced 3D game development, Panda3D stands out as a formidable option. This engine, originally developed by Disney for its own game projects, is now open-source and widely supported by a robust community.

Panda3D is known for its powerful rendering capabilities and ease of use, allowing developers to bring their immersive 3D environments and characters to life with Python's simplicity and readability.

Another notable engine is Godot, which has gained significant traction for both 2D and 3D game development. While Godot uses its own scripting language, GDScript, designed to resemble Python's syntax closely, it offers excellent support for Python through various third-party modules. This makes Godot an attractive option for Python developers looking to leverage their existing skills in a versatile and user-friendly engine.

Blender, primarily known for its capabilities as a 3D modeling and animation tool, also includes a built-in game engine. This unique combination allows developers to design, model, and animate their games within a single software package. Python acts as the scripting language for game logic within Blender, making it an integrated tool for developers interested in both game development and 3D design.

Ursina Engine, although a newer entrant into the game development scene, is specifically designed for Python 3. Its focus is on ease of use, making game development accessible to beginners while not sacrificing the depth needed for more complex projects. Ursina relies heavily on Python's syntax and principals to empower developers in creating 3D games efficiently.

When choosing a game engine, it's crucial to consider the project's specific needs, including the type of game you are developing, the level of complexity you aim to achieve, and your own proficiency in Python. Each engine comes with its own set of strengths and learning curves, and the best choice varies based on individual project requirements and developer preferences.

Engaging with the community is also a vital part of working with game engines. Communities can offer support, tutorials, plugins, and templates that can significantly speed up the development process. Many of these engines have active forums and user groups focused on Python development, providing an invaluable resource for troubleshooting and innovation.

Beyond the engines mentioned, there are several other tools and libraries in Python geared towards game development. These include Cocos2d for 2D games, Kivy for mobile and multi-touch applications, and PyOpenGL for working directly with OpenGL in creating 3D graphics. The choice of tools greatly depends on the project's requirements and the developer's comfort with Python.

Documentation and tutorials play a crucial role in learning these engines and libraries. Fortunately, the Python community has contributed a wealth of resources to help developers start their game development journey. From written guides and API references to video tutorials and example projects, there's no shortage of learning materials available online.

Experimentation and practice are key to mastering these engines. Starting with simpler projects and gradually increasing complexity can help solidify your understanding of both Python and the game development process. Each project presents an opportunity to explore different facets of game development, from physics and collision detection to AI and multiplayer functionality.

Game development with Python also offers the chance to understand the importance of performance optimization. As games often require real-time performance, learning how to optimize code and use resources efficiently becomes crucial. This can include everything from managing game loops and handling events to understanding the nuances of graphics rendering and network latency.

Finally, the landscape of game engines compatible with Python continues to evolve. New tools and libraries emerge, and existing ones get updates and improvements. Staying connected with the community and keeping an eye on the latest trends and technologies is important for keeping your skills up-to-date and taking advantage of what the Python ecosystem has to offer for game development.

In conclusion, Python's versatility and the rich ecosystem of game engines and libraries make it an excellent choice for both 2D and 3D game development. Whether you're a beginner looking to create your first game or an experienced developer aiming to leverage Python's strengths in game development, there's a tool out there that fits your needs. By exploring these engines, engaging with the community, and continuously learning, you can unlock the full potential of Python for creating engaging, impactful games.

Building a Simple Game from Scratch

The allure of crafting an entire world within the realm of computer code is an ambition shared by many programmers. Within this chapter, we will embark on the journey of building a simple game from scratch using Python. This endeavor amalgamates the basics of Python programming with the fascinating prospects of game development. It serves as a practical application of previously discussed topics and introduces the reader to the concept of game loops, event handling, and graphical output using Pygame—a popular set of Python modules designed for writing video games.

Our first step is to ensure that the Pygame library is installed. Pygame acts as a foundation, abstracting away the complexities of direct graphics and sound manipulation. This allows us to focus on the game logic rather than the intricacies of the operating system. Installation can be easily achieved through pip, Python's package manager, by running the command **pip install pygame** in the terminal or command prompt.

With Pygame installed, we begin by importing Pygame into our project and initializing it. This process prepares the necessary components for audio and video outputs. The code snippet **import pygame**
pygame.init() signifies the beginning of our game's codebase. Each game developed with Pygame requires these lines to ensure the library is properly set up.

Next, we focus on creating the game window. Pygame allows for the easy configuration of a window where our game's visual elements will be displayed. By specifying dimensions, we can create a canvas for our imagination. A typical window can be created with the following lines:

```
screen = pygame.display.set_mode((800, 600))
pygame.display.set_caption("My Game")
```

This code snippet not only establishes a window with the dimensions of 800 pixels in width and 600 pixels in height but also sets a title for the window. Creating a visually appealing title screen is the first step in engaging the player.

Moving forward, we delve into the main loop of the game. The game loop is a critical concept, it keeps the game running by continuously checking for events (such as keystrokes and mouse movements), updating game states, and rendering graphics. A basic structure of a game loop in Pygame looks like this:

```
running = True
while running:
for event in pygame.event.get():
if event.type == pygame.QUIT:
running = False
pygame.display.flip()
pygame.quit()
```

This loop continues to run, keeping our game active until the **running** variable is set to False, which occurs when the user closes the game window.

Let's enrich our game by adding a background color and drawing shapes. Pygame facilitates this through simple methods such as **screen.fill(color)** and **pygame.draw.circle(screen, color, position, radius)**. These functions alter the visual output, allowing us to design the game setting and objects involved.

Interaction is a vital aspect of gaming. Pygame processes events such as key presses and mouse clicks, making game characters respond to user inputs. Through conditional statements within the main loop, we can detect specific keys being pressed and move a character or object accordingly.

Envisioning a simple game where the objective is to dodge incoming obstacles, we introduce a player character in the form of a sprite. Pygame simplifies sprite management with classes that support animations and movements. By extending the **pygame.sprite.Sprite** class, we can create our player with abilities to move across the screen.

As our game evolves, adding obstacles and a scoring system becomes necessary. Pygame accommodates collision detection, which we can utilize to determine when the player sprite collides with an obstacle sprite. An increase in score for avoiding collisions and a game over scenario upon collision can be implemented to provide challenge and progression.

Sound effects and background music significantly enhance the gaming experience. Pygame allows for the easy addition of audio through its mixer module. Loading and playing sounds when certain actions occur, like a score increase or game over, can be achieved with minimal code.

To conclude our simple game, we incorporate a method to exit cleanly and a mechanism to display the score on screen. Pygame provides fonts and text rendering capabilities to show the score, and the **pygame.quit()** method ensures resources are properly released when the game closes.

In essence, building a game from scratch, as demonstrated, provides a hands-on approach to understanding game development concepts while showcasing the versatility of Python. It accentuates the joy of seeing one's code come to life in the form of interactive entertainment. Remember, the game developed in this chapter is rudimentary. The world of game development with Python is vast, with endless possibilities to explore. As skills and knowledge advance, more complex and visually impressive games can be built, reinforcing Python's position as a formidable tool in the programmer's arsenal.

Embrace the creativity that game development with Python unlocks. Experiment with different game ideas, mechanics, and Pygame features. Challenge yourself with additional functionalities like multi-player capabilities or integration with web services for high scores. The journey from a simple game to complex creations begins with the foundational skills covered in this chapter. Let this be the stepping stone to your adventure in Python game development.

Chapter 22: Python in Finance and Fintech

In today's rapidly evolving financial landscape, Python has emerged as a linchpin in the realms of finance and fintech. Its simplicity and robust ecosystem make it an ideal choice for professionals seeking to harness computational methods to analyze markets, predict trends, and automate trading. As we delve into this chapter, we will explore the critical role that Python plays in algorithmic trading, where it is used to develop models that can process large volumes of data in real time to make trading decisions automatically. Moreover, our journey will take us through the intricacies of financial analysis and modeling, showcasing how Python's libraries like pandas and NumPy transform complex financial datasets into actionable insights.

Additionally, the surge of interest in cryptocurrencies and blockchain technology has opened new avenues for Python programmers. This chapter will touch upon how Python's versatility and the availability of specialized libraries facilitate the development of applications for blockchain, contributing to secure and transparent financial transactions. Whether you are interested in automating your investment portfolio, analyzing financial markets, or developing cutting-edge fintech applications, this chapter will equip you with the foundational knowledge and skills to advance in the finance sector using Python. By the end of this chapter, learners at all levels will appreciate Python's potential to innovate and drive progress in the fintech industry.

Algorithmic Trading with Python

Algorithmic trading, a method where computers make trade orders based on predefined criteria, has significantly grown in popularity within the finance sector. Python, known for its simplicity and powerful libraries, has become a favored programming language among traders and financial engineers to develop these automated trading systems. This section aims to introduce the concept of algorithmic trading and guide on how to utilize Python to harness its potential.

At the core of algorithmic trading is the idea that by analyzing market data through mathematical models, one can identify profitable trading opportunities. Python, with libraries like NumPy, pandas, and Matplotlib, provides a robust environment for data analysis and visualization, making it perfect for such tasks. Moreover, Python's simplicity allows for the rapid development and testing of complex algorithms without a steep learning curve.

Before diving into the coding aspect, it's essential to understand the financial instruments commonly traded algorithmically. These include stocks, futures, options, and foreign exchange. Each has its own set of characteristics and market behaviors; thus, the strategies developed should be tailored accordingly. Python's versatility allows developers to easily adjust and experiment with different models and strategies for these instruments.

The first step in algorithmic trading with Python is data collection. Market data, which can be historical or real-time, is necessary for strategy development and testing. Python facilitates data collection through APIs provided by data vendors and trading platforms. The use of libraries like Requests to access these APIs and pandas for data manipulation makes it straightforward to fetch, process, and analyze market data.

After collecting the needed data, the next step is to develop a trading strategy. This involves applying statistical and mathematical models to identify potential trades. Python's rich ecosystem includes libraries such as SciPy and Statsmodels, which offer a wide range of statistical functions that aid in strategy development. Whether it's simple moving average strategies or complex machine learning models, Python provides the necessary tools to create, test, and implement them.

Backtesting is a critical process in algorithmic trading. It involves simulating a trading strategy using historical data to assess its viability. Python's pandas library, with its efficient data structures, allows for the easy manipulation and analysis of financial time series data, making backtests both accurate and efficient. Frameworks like Backtrader and PyAlgoTrade offer extensive functionality specifically designed for backtesting, including support for various data sources and performance metrics.

Once a strategy has been backtested and refined, the next phase is implementation. Execution of trades in a live market requires careful handling to minimize costs and slippage. Again, Python comes to the rescue with packages like ccxt for cryptocurrency or ibpy for interactive brokers, which provide interfaces to connect with brokerage platforms and execute trades programmatically.

Risk management is another aspect where Python's capabilities shine. By employing Python's numerical libraries, traders can build models to calculate the risk associated with their portfolios and adjust their strategies based on real-time market conditions. This proactive approach to risk management is crucial in safeguarding investments from significant losses.

Performance measurement is vital to evaluate how a trading strategy performs over time. Python's libraries offer comprehensive tools for calculating various performance metrics such as Sharpe ratio, drawdowns, and return on investment. These metrics are indispensable for fine-tuning strategies and making informed decisions.

It's worth noting that while Python significantly lowers the barrier to entry for algorithmic trading, success in this field requires a deep understanding of both the financial markets and the algorithms being deployed. Continuous learning and adaptation to market changes are crucial for maintaining a competitive edge.

One of the beauties of Python in algorithmic trading is the extensive community support. Numerous forums, tutorials, and open-source projects are available for learning and sharing knowledge. Newcomers and experienced developers alike will find a wealth of resources to help them on their journey.

For those interested in exploring algorithmic trading further, it's recommended to start small with simple strategies and slowly scale up. Experimentation is key, and Python's flexibility and ease of use make it an excellent tool for this purpose. As you gain more experience, you may delve into machine learning models to predict market movements or explore high-frequency trading techniques.

Lastly, ethical considerations and regulatory compliance are crucial in algorithmic trading. Developers must ensure their algorithms do not engage in market manipulation or other unethical behaviors. Python's ability to quickly prototype and test can be used to ensure compliance with these regulations.

In conclusion, Python's simplicity, along with its powerful libraries, makes it an ideal programming language for developing algorithmic trading strategies. Whether you're a beginner or an experienced developer, Python provides the tools necessary to analyze market data, backtest strategies, and execute trades. By understanding the fundamentals outlined in this section and continuously learning, you can unlock the potential of algorithmic trading and possibly achieve significant success in the financial markets.

Emerging trends in financial technology continue to provide new opportunities for algorithmic traders. As Python evolves, so too will the strategies and tools available for finance professionals. Keeping up with these advancements will ensure that your skills and knowledge remain relevant in this fast-paced domain.

Financial Analysis and Modeling

In the rapidly evolving landscape of finance and fintech, Python has emerged as a fundamental tool owing to its simplicity and powerful libraries dedicated to data analysis and manipulation. Financial analysis and modeling, pivotal in crafting investment strategies, risk management, and financial planning, greatly benefit from Python's capabilities.

At the heart of financial analysis lies the ability to compute statistical measures, predict market trends, and analyze historical data. Python, with libraries such as Pandas and NumPy, simplifies these tasks by allowing analysts to work with large datasets efficiently. Moreover, the Matplotlib library offers the means to visualize data and analytical results through graphs and charts, making complex information more accessible and comprehensible.

Financial modeling, an intricate exercise that forecasts a company's financial performance, also finds a robust supporter in Python. Through models, analysts draw insights that inform investment decisions and policy formulation. Python facilitates this process with tools that automate the generation of financial statements and valuation models, yielding quicker and more reliable outcomes.

Understanding Python's role in finance requires familiarity with its ecosystem of libraries. Pandas, for example, is indispensable for data manipulation tasks like cleaning, filling, or omitting gaps in data. This cleanliness is crucial in finance, where even minor errors can lead to significant misjudgments.

NumPy enriches the Python financial toolkit by adding support for complex mathematical functions and multi-dimensional arrays. It enables analysts to perform high-level mathematical computations necessary for creating sophisticated quantitative models.

When it comes to visualization, Matplotlib and Seaborn make data interpretation visually intuitive. Seaborn, building on Matplotlib, introduces more themes and visualization patterns, which are especially useful in presenting financial data trends and distributions in a more refined and attractive manner.

Financial analysis isn't just about handling existing data; it's also about predicting future trends. Here, Python's Scikit-learn library comes into play, offering machine learning algorithms for predictive modeling. By applying these algorithms, analysts can forecast stock prices, interest rates, and much more with a degree of precision that was hard to achieve manually.

Python's utility in financial analysis and modeling is also evident in risk management. Libraries like TensorFlow and PyRisk are tailored for constructing models that assess and mitigate risks. They help in analyzing market volatility and the probability of adverse financial outcomes, thereby guiding strategy to avoid potential losses.

Quantitative finance is another area where Python has carved out a significant niche. In quant finance, Python scripts are used for algorithmic trading, options pricing, and asset allocation strategies. The ability to process and analyze vast quantities of data at high speed makes Python ideal for these high-stakes applications.

While diving into financial modeling with Python, it's crucial to understand the underlying financial theories and principles. Python acts as a tool that amplifies the analysts' capabilities, but the foundational knowledge of finance is indispensable. This knowledge, combined with Python skills, enables the creation of accurate and insightful financial models.

For beginners in Python, starting with simple financial calculations and progressively advancing towards building complex models is a practical approach. This journey enhances both their programming and financial analytics skills simultaneously. Practical projects, such as predicting stock prices or analyzing corporate financial health, can serve as excellent learning paths.

Documentation and reproducibility are critical aspects of financial analysis and modeling. Python aids this through well-structured code and the use of Jupyter Notebooks. Jupyter Notebooks allow for the presentation of code, outputs, and narrative explanations in a single document, making it easier to share insights and methodologies with others.

One of the most appealing aspects of using Python for financial analysis is the strong community and plethora of resources available. From forums like Stack Overflow to specialized communities focused on Python in finance, newcomers and seasoned professionals alike can find guidance, share knowledge, and collaborate on projects.

Finally, security and compliance cannot be overlooked. Python's libraries and frameworks offer support in ensuring that financial applications are secure and meet the regulatory standards imposed by financial authorities. This support underscores Python's suitability for sensitive financial operations.

In conclusion, Python's relevance in financial analysis and modeling cannot be overstated. Its comprehensive suite of libraries and tools, combined with its simplicity and versatility, makes it a powerhouse for financial professionals. Whether it's conducting analyses, creating models, or predicting future trends, Python has established itself as an indispensable resource in the finance and fintech sectors.

Python in Blockchain and Cryptocurrency

As the digital economy grows, the interconnection between Python and the innovative landscapes of blockchain and cryptocurrency becomes increasingly significant. Python's versatility and ease of use have made it a popular choice among blockchain developers and crypto enthusiasts. In this section, we will explore the integrative role Python plays within these cutting-edge technologies.

Blockchain technology, at its core, is a decentralized database or ledger that records transactions across multiple computers in a way that ensures the security, transparency, and immutability of the data. Python, with its straightforward syntax, enables developers to build blockchain applications succinctly and efficiently. The simplicity of Python allows for a more accessible understanding of the complex algorithms that underpin blockchain technology.

Cryptocurrency, a blockchain's most famous application, has transformed the way we perceive and use money. Python's role in cryptocurrency goes beyond mere financial transactions; it extends into areas such as building trading bots, developing decentralized applications (dApps), and analyzing the cryptocurrency market. Python libraries such as Pandas and NumPy have become integral in processing and analyzing the vast amounts of data generated by cryptocurrency markets.

One of the key aspects of blockchain development is the creation of smart contracts. These are self-executing contracts with the terms of the agreement directly written into lines of code. Python, through frameworks such as Ethereum's Vyper, offers an environment to develop these contracts in a more secure and intuitive manner compared to other programming languages.

Moreover, Python's extensive suite of libraries and frameworks simplifies the development process of decentralized applications (dApps). Libraries like Web3.py allow developers to interact with Ethereum, enabling them to build and automate the deployment of dApps directly from Python scripts. This synergy between Python and blockchain technologies enhances the development landscape, making it more efficient and accessible.

Regarding cryptocurrency trading, Python has emerged as a key tool in the development of trading algorithms and bots. The flexibility of Python enables traders to automate their strategies, backtest historical data, and execute trades in real-time. Libraries such as CCXT provide a unified way of accessing cryptocurrency markets across multiple exchanges, simplifying the process of algorithmic trading.

Data analysis and visualization play a crucial role in the cryptocurrency market. Python's data analysis libraries, such as Pandas and Matplotlib, offer powerful tools for analyzing trends, market movements, and blockchain transactions. This capacity for robust data analysis makes Python indispensable for individuals and institutions looking to make data-driven decisions in the cryptocurrency space.

Security is paramount in the realm of blockchain and cryptocurrency. Python's contribution to this aspect is noteworthy, with libraries like hashlib and PyCrypto that provide cryptographic services, enhancing the security of blockchain applications. This includes the generation of secure keys, encryption and decryption of data, and the creation of digital signatures.

In the burgeoning field of Non-Fungible Tokens (NFTs), Python is making its mark as well. Through various Python libraries and APIs, developers can mint, transfer, and manage NFTs on blockchain platforms. This opens up new avenues for Python developers in the realm of digital art, collectibles, and beyond.

Education and community support further strengthen Python's position in blockchain and cryptocurrency. Numerous online resources, courses, and community forums are dedicated to exploring the use of Python in these technologies, making it easier for newcomers to enter the field and for professionals to stay updated with the latest developments.

Challenges such as scalability, transaction speed, and energy consumption are at the forefront of blockchain development. Python developers are actively involved in projects aimed at addressing these challenges, contributing to a more sustainable and efficient blockchain infrastructure.

As the landscape of blockchain and cryptocurrency continues to evolve, the adaptability and innovation within the Python community will play a crucial role in shaping its future. From experimenting with new blockchain protocols to enhancing the scalability of cryptocurrencies, Python's role is fundamental in driving forward these technological advancements.

Finally, the emergence of decentralized finance (DeFi) and smart contracts has unveiled new possibilities for automating and decentralizing financial services. Python stands as a bridge for finance professionals venturing into the world of blockchain, offering the tools and frameworks necessary for developing and deploying DeFi applications.

In conclusion, Python's influence in the realm of blockchain and cryptocurrency is both profound and multifaceted. Its ease of use, combined with powerful libraries and a supportive community, positions Python as an essential tool for developers, traders, and analysts in the blockchain and cryptocurrency sectors. As these technologies continue to grow and evolve, Python's role is set to become even more significant, offering endless possibilities for innovation and development.

The exploration of Python in blockchain and cryptocurrency reveals a promising integration of programming expertise with the next generation of financial and technological innovation. For developers, understanding Python's capabilities in this sphere is not just about coding, but about contributing to the future of decentralized technologies. As we move forward, the collaboration between Python and blockchain will undoubtedly lead to more secure, efficient, and innovative solutions in the digital economy.

Chapter 23: Python in Education and Academic Research

In the vast arena of education and academic research, Python emerges as a powerful and versatile tool, bridging the gap between beginners' learning curves and experts' need for advanced computation. This chapter delves into Python's role as a cornerstone in the educational domain, highlighting its efficacy in simplifying programming concepts for newcomers while offering robust libraries and frameworks for complex scientific computing. The significance of Python in academia is underscored by its prevalence in scientific research, where it facilitates data analysis, simulation, and visualization tasks, thereby accelerating the pace of discovery and innovation. Furthermore, collaborative research efforts are increasingly empowered by tools such as Jupyter Notebooks, which permit the sharing of code, results, and explanatory notes in a cohesive document, fostering an environment of transparency and collective knowledge building. Through these discussions, it becomes evident that Python's simplicity, alongside its comprehensive ecosystem, not only makes it an ideal teaching tool but also a pivotal enabler in pushing the boundaries of academic research.

Python as a Teaching Tool

In the realm of education, Python emerges not merely as a programming language but as a versatile instrument, welding simplicity and efficacy. It's pivotal to delve into why and how Python has become a cornerstone in the edifice of academic and instructional methodologies. As we voyage through this examination, we uncover Python's strategic application across diverse educational landscapes, aiming to enrich, empower, and elucidate.

At the heart of Python's educational adoption is its uncluttered syntax, closely mirroring human language. This characteristic diminishes the intimidating barrier to entry for programming novices. Where other languages might ensnare learners in syntactical intricacies, Python escorts them gently into the world of programming, making it an ideal teaching tool for introductory programming courses across high schools and universities.

Furthermore, Python's versatility spans multiple domains, from web development to data analysis, offering students a broad spectrum of application areas. This not only sustains their engagement but also broadens their perspective on potential career paths. Such versatility ensures that the skills students acquire are not just academic exercises but are readily applicable in real-world scenarios.

Another dimension of Python's educational value is its extensive library ecosystem. Libraries such as NumPy and Pandas for data analysis, Matplotlib for data visualization, and Django for web development, allow learners to extend their basic programming skills into specialized areas with relative ease. This access to a wide array of tools encourages experimentation and fosters a deeper understanding of programming concepts.

Python's role in education extends beyond individual learning into collaborative academic research. It serves as a lingua franca in interdisciplinary research teams, where specialists in fields as diverse as biology, economics, and engineering can share and develop code. This universality enhances collaboration, allowing for the seamless integration of diverse expertise in tackling complex research questions.

On the pedagogical front, Python facilitates an active learning environment. Its compatibility with interactive platforms like Jupyter Notebooks enables educators to blend explanatory text, live code, and visualizations into comprehensive learning resources. These interactive notebooks have revolutionized how programming is taught, moving away from passive lectures to engaging, hands-on sessions.

Thanks to Python's simplicity, educators are empowered to focus on teaching computational thinking—a set of problem-solving skills critical in the digital age—without getting bogged down by language-specific details. This shift towards developing a computational mindset prepares students not just for immediate programming challenges but for a lifetime of logical thinking and problem-solving.

Moreover, Python's open-source nature fosters a culture of sharing and collaboration. Numerous educational resources, from textbooks to online tutorials, are freely available, significantly lowering the barriers to high-quality education materials. This open-access model has been instrumental in democratizing programming education, making learning resources available to a global audience.

Institutionally, the adoption of Python is also facilitated by its cost-effectiveness. Being open-source, it eliminates the financial constraints associated with proprietary software, making it an attractive option for educational institutions operating under tight budgets. This economic feasibility, combined with Python's powerful capabilities, has contributed to its widespread integration into curriculums worldwide.

The inclusivity that Python promotes is also noteworthy. Its community values and robust support networks provide a welcoming environment for underrepresented groups in tech. Programming clubs, online forums, and global events like PyCon engage learners from diverse backgrounds, fostering a sense of belonging and encouragement.

Innovations in teaching methodologies have also been enabled by Python's adaptability. For instance, gamified learning environments where Python is used to solve puzzles or build games, captivate students' interests, making learning both fun and effective. These novel approaches address various learning styles, ensuring a more inclusive and effective educational process.

Python's role is pivotal in the burgeoning field of machine learning and artificial intelligence education. Its libraries, such as TensorFlow and Keras, have become standard tools for introducing students to these advanced technologies. By learning Python, students gain access to cutting-edge fields, ensuring they are equipped with the knowledge and skills demanded by industry and academia alike.

The anecdotal success stories of learners who began their programming journey with Python further underscore its efficacy as a teaching tool. From young enthusiasts creating their first projects to researchers solving complex problems, Python's impact is profound and far-reaching. These narratives not only inspire but also highlight Python's role in sparking and sustaining a lifelong interest in programming.

In conclusion, Python's ascendancy as a preferred teaching tool in education is a testament to its simplicity, versatility, and supportive community. It not only lowers entry barriers for beginners but also opens up a universe of possibilities for advanced learners and researchers. As Python continues to evolve, its contribution to education is expected to grow even further, shaping the next generation of programmers, scientists, and innovators.

Embracing Python in education is not just about teaching a programming language; it's about nurturing problem solvers who are prepared to tackle the challenges of tomorrow. This intrinsic value of Python elevates it from a tool to an essential component of contemporary education, equipping learners not just with coding skills but with a mindset geared towards innovation and exploration.

Python for Scientific Computing

In the realm of scientific computing, Python has emerged as a cornerstone, revolutionizing how research is conducted, data is analyzed, and findings are elucidated. The ascendancy of Python in this domain can be attributed to its simplicity, versatility, and the extensive ecosystem of libraries and tools it supports. Scientific computing encompasses a broad range of activities, from numerical analysis and modeling to simulations and data processing. At its core, it seeks to harness computational methodologies to solve complex scientific problems, enabling researchers to transcend the traditional boundaries of theoretical and empirical methods.

One of the keystones of Python's utility in scientific computing is its array of libraries specialized for mathematical operations, data analysis, and visualization. Libraries such as NumPy and SciPy provide the backbone for numerical computations, offering efficient implementations of mathematical routines that are both robust and easily accessible. These libraries are not just tools but gateways, bridging the gap between the intricate world of scientific theory and the practical realm of computational application. They allow for operations on large datasets and matrices with syntax that is intuitive and grounded in the mathematical notation familiar to researchers.

Moreover, Python's role in data analysis within scientific research cannot be overstated. Libraries like pandas have set the standard for data manipulation and analysis, offering data structures and operations that streamline the process of exploring, cleaning, and transforming data. Pandas, in combination with Python's powerful data visualization libraries such as Matplotlib and Seaborn, enable researchers to uncover insights from data through sophisticated visual representations. These tools collectively empower scientists to articulate complex data patterns and relationships in a clear and impactful manner.

The realms of machine learning and artificial intelligence also fall within the ambit of scientific computing, where Python again stands out. Frameworks such as TensorFlow and Scikit-learn have facilitated the development and implementation of machine learning models, propelling forward areas such as predictive analytics, natural language processing, and image recognition. These technologies not only augment the capabilities of scientific research but also open avenues for interdisciplinary investigations, melding the computational with the conceptual.

Python's ascendancy in scientific computing is further bolstered by its high degree of interoperability with other programming languages and tools. This interconnectivity enables researchers to integrate Python into a wider toolchain, leveraging the strengths of various technologies. For instance, Python can interface with R for statistical analysis or MATLAB for engineering applications, creating a cohesive ecosystem that is flexible and powerful.

The significance of reproducibility in scientific research cannot be understated, and here too, Python makes a substantial contribution. The use of Jupyter Notebooks, an interactive computational environment, has transformed how scientists document and share their research. These notebooks allow for the dissemination of research that is not only readable but also executable, encompassing code, equations, visualizations, and narrative text. This fosters a culture of openness and collaboration, essential pillars in the advancement of scientific knowledge.

Education and academic research have greatly benefitted from Python's capabilities in scientific computing. Its syntax is clear and concise, making Python an excellent tool for teaching computational science and programming. Students learning Python can apply their skills in real-world scientific research projects, thereby bridging the gap between theoretical knowledge and practical application. This hands-on experience is invaluable, cultivating a new generation of researchers who are proficient in both their scientific disciplines and in computational methodologies.

The development of custom scientific applications is another area where Python shines. Researchers can leverage Python to build bespoke applications tailored to their unique requirements. These can range from simulations and models to data analysis pipelines and more. The flexibility of Python, coupled with its extensive libraries, means that the possibilities are virtually limitless, enabling innovative approaches to scientific inquiry.

The role of Python in the simulation of natural and engineered systems deserves special mention. Through libraries such as PySPH for particle-based simulations or FEniCS for solving differential equations, Python facilitates the modeling of complex systems. This capability is crucial across many scientific disciplines, from physics and chemistry to biology and engineering, assisting researchers in understanding phenomena that are difficult or impossible to observe directly.

Scientific communities have embraced Python not only for its technical merits but also for the ethos of collaboration and sharing it promotes. The open-source nature of Python and its libraries encourages a model of development where tools are continuously improved and extended by the community. This collaborative spirit accelerates the pace of innovation and ensures that cutting-edge computational techniques are accessible to all.

Moreover, Python's role extends beyond traditional scientific realms into emerging fields such as bioinformatics, geoinformatics, and social sciences. The flexibility and breadth of Python's scientific stack enable it to adapt to the unique computational needs of these disciplines. Whether it's analyzing genomic sequences or modeling climate change impacts, Python provides the tools that empower researchers to tackle the pressing challenges of our time.

The future of Python in scientific computing looks promising. As computational power continues to grow and datasets become ever larger and more complex, Python's role is likely to expand. The development of new libraries and tools, driven by the needs of researchers and the innovation of the community, will further enhance Python's capabilities. This ongoing evolution will ensure that Python remains at the forefront of scientific computing, helping to unravel the mysteries of the universe and improve our understanding of the world around us.

In conclusion, Python for scientific computing is a testament to the language's versatility and power. It serves as a bridge between the abstract and the empirical, enabling researchers to explore new frontiers in science and technology. Through its comprehensive libraries, community support, and ease of learning, Python has democratized scientific computing, making it accessible to researchers, students, and enthusiasts around the globe. As we look to the future, Python's role in scientific discovery and education is set to grow, continuing to shape how we understand and interact with the world.

For beginners to advanced programmers, understanding Python's application in scientific computing is not just about mastering a tool; it's about unlocking a world of possibilities. It challenges us to think differently about problem-solving and provides a robust platform for innovation and discovery. As we delve into Python's capabilities in scientific computing, we're reminded of the profound impact that computing has had on scientific progress and the potential it holds for shaping our future.

Collaborative Research with Jupyter Notebooks

In the realm of academic research and education, Python has risen as a beacon of innovation and productivity, enabling students, educators, and researchers to push the boundaries of knowledge through both theoretical and applied sciences. Among the tools that have significantly bolstered this endeavor, Jupyter Notebooks stand out as a critical asset in collaborative research environments.

Jupyter Notebooks offer an interactive computing environment where users can combine live code, equations, visualizations, and narrative text into a single document. This unique capability makes it an invaluable tool for conducting research that is not only rigorous but also comprehensible and reproducible. The essence of Jupyter Notebooks lies in its support for code execution right beside the explanations and data visualizations, providing an integrated data analysis workflow.

The integration of Python into Jupyter Notebooks has been a game-changer for those engaged in data-intensive research fields such as data science, machine learning, computational biology, and many others. Python's simplicity and powerful ecosystem, encompassing libraries like NumPy, Pandas, Matplotlib, and SciPy, enable researchers to handle complex data analysis tasks with relative ease.

One of the most compelling features of Jupyter Notebooks for collaborative research is its ability to seamlessly blend code with narrative. This encourages a practice where researchers can not only share their code and findings but also the thought process and methodologies underlying their research. It's a digital lab notebook that's perfect for sharing insights with colleagues, or for teaching purposes where elucidation of complex concepts is necessary.

Collaboration in research entails combining the efforts of various individuals to contribute towards a shared goal. Jupyter Notebooks facilitate this by being easily shareable and accessible through platforms like GitHub or even JupyterHub. Herein, researchers can share their notebooks for peer review, allowing others to execute the code independently, verify results, and perhaps even suggest enhancements or identify issues.

The role of Jupyter Notebooks in education, particularly in fields requiring extensive computation, cannot be overstated. It allows instructors to create interactive lecture notes that students can run on their own computers. Such interactive notes can contain exercises that students can complete and submit electronically, making the learning experience more engaging and hands-on.

Version control systems, notably Git, when used in conjunction with Jupyter Notebooks, further enhance the collaborative capabilities by tracking changes over time. This allows research teams to work on different sections of a project simultaneously, merge their work, and resolve conflicts that arise from concurrent modifications. It's an elaborate dance of synchronization, but it enables a more dynamic and flexible approach to research projects.

Executing experiments and analyzing data in real-time is yet another strength of using Jupyter Notebooks in research. They can be connected to a large variety of data sources and can leverage cloud computing resources, making it possible to process large datasets that would be impractical on personal computers. The interactive nature of notebooks makes it easier to test hypotheses, perform exploratory data analysis, and visualize results dynamically.

Despite the numerous benefits, working collaboratively on Jupyter Notebooks also comes with its set of challenges. The linear narrative structure of notebooks can sometimes make merging changes difficult, especially if multiple users edit the same section of a notebook simultaneously. Researchers need to adopt strategies such as clear communication, delineation of tasks, and regular synchronization to mitigate these issues.

Moreover, the reproducibility of research findings through Jupyter Notebooks requires careful attention to detail. This includes ensuring that all dependencies are correctly specified and that the notebook environment can be replicated. Tools like Docker, along with the practice of sharing notebooks with embedded data and figures, can significantly enhance reproducibility.

For those concerned about the presentation of their research, Jupyter Notebooks support conversion to a range of formats including HTML, PDF, and slides, facilitating the dissemination of work in formats suitable for different audiences. This conversion feature is especially useful for researchers preparing their findings for conferences, journal publications, or teaching materials.

On top of everything, the Jupyter Notebook's support for interactive widgets allows the creation of GUI elements, such as sliders and buttons, within the notebook. This can be used to develop interactive demonstrations of algorithms, making research findings more accessible and understandable to a broader audience.

In summary, Jupyter Notebooks embody a powerful platform for collaborative research in the academic sphere, leveraging the versatility of Python. They provide an ecosystem where data analysis, reproducibility, and collaboration converge to facilitate innovative research. While challenges in collaboration exist, the benefits of using Jupyter Notebooks for academic research are profound, leading to deeper insights and more effective educational outcomes.

As we continue to explore the use of Python in education and academic research, it's clear that tools like Jupyter Notebooks are indispensable in the modern researcher's toolkit. Embracing these tools requires an understanding of both their potential and their limitations.

Nevertheless, with the continued growth and support of the Python community, these challenges can be addressed, paving the way for a new era of collaborative discovery and learning.

Chapter 24: Creative Coding and Art with Python

As we delve into Chapter 24, we transition from the utilitarian aspects of Python to explore its capabilities in creative coding and art. This realm combines the precision of computer science with the boundlessness of artistic vision, allowing Python programmers to extend their skills beyond traditional applications. The chapter begins by illustrating how Python can be harnessed for music and sound generation, revealing methods to synthesize new sounds or manipulate existing ones, thus opening a vast playground for sonic experimentation. Moving forward, we explore the generation of art and visualizations, a segment that not only demonstrates Python's ability to create complex graphics and animations but also its power in data visualization, making abstract data comprehensibly beautiful. Furthermore, we delve into Python-based tools for digital content creation, which encompasses a wide range of activities from video editing to 3D modeling, underscoring Python's versatility and its growing prominence in the digital arts sphere. Engaging with this chapter, enthusiasts at any skill level - from beginners to advanced coders - will discover the joy of blending coding with creativity, ultimately expanding the horizon of what they can achieve with Python.

Python in Music and Sound Generation

The intersection of Python and music is a realm where technical know-how meets creative exploration. This convergence enables both beginners and advanced practitioners to generate music, process audio, and even create new instruments. Python, with its extensive libraries and straightforward syntax, has become a pivotal tool in the digital audio landscape.

One of the primary libraries for music and sound generation in Python is PyDub. PyDub is immensely popular for its ability to manipulate audio with a simple and Pythonic set of commands. Users can cut, concatenate, and alter audio files with ease. For those stepping into the world of digital music production, understanding PyDub's functionality provides a strong foundation.

Another significant library is music21, a tool designed for musicology. music21 analyzes music in various formats and generates musical scores. This library bridges the gap between computational analysis and practical music theory, making it an invaluable asset for researchers and musicians alike.

For synthesizing sounds and creating music in real-time, Pyo stands out. It offers a plethora of features for audio processing and synthesis. Pyo allows users to craft their digital instruments, making it a playground for sound designers and electronic musicians. The library's comprehensive documentation and tutorials support users in pushing the boundaries of digital sound.

The Sonic Pi, though not a Python library, deserves mention for its influence on the Python ecosystem. Inspired by Sonic Pi's design, projects such as FoxDot and PyLive have emerged, allowing Python programmers to live code music. These tools facilitate a performance style where coding and composition merge, showcasing Python's versatility.

Audio analysis is another area where Python shines. Libraries like LibROSA offer tools for music and audio analysis, including beat tracking, pitch detection, and more. These capabilities are crucial for tasks ranging from automatic music transcription to building recommendation systems for streaming services.

In education, Python's role in music generation demystifies the process of creating music with code. By introducing students to programming through the lens of music, educators foster a multidisciplinary approach to learning. Python's syntax is accessible for beginners, making it an excellent choice for integrating coding and music in the classroom.

The integration of MIDI (Musical Instrument Digital Interface) with Python opens another avenue for musical exploration. Utilizing libraries such as Mido, programmers can send and receive MIDI signals, interact with hardware instruments, and even create their virtual synthesizers. This interaction with hardware brings a tangible aspect to Python's musical capabilities.

Machine learning, a rapidly growing area within Python, has profound implications for music and sound generation. Libraries like TensorFlow and PyTorch enable the creation of models that can generate music autonomously, learn from existing compositions, and even imitate the styles of famous musicians. The fusion of AI and music through Python paves the way for innovative compositions and research.

The open-source nature of Python and its libraries encourages collaboration and sharing within the music tech community. Platforms like GitHub host numerous projects where musicians and developers work together to create new instruments, effects, and techniques for music generation. This collaborative spirit accelerates the evolution of Python in music.

Performance and efficiency are considerations when using Python for real-time audio processing. While Python might not always match the speed of lower-level languages, techniques such as using Cython or optimizing critical parts of the code ensure that Python remains a viable option for music production.

Exploring the vast landscape of Python in music and sound generation reveals a community where innovation flourishes. From generating new compositions to analyzing classic pieces, Python serves as a bridge between the analytical and the artistic. Its role in music technology continues to grow, reflecting the language's flexibility and the creativity of its users.

As we consider the future of Python in music, it's clear that the community will drive its evolution. New libraries and tools will emerge, refining and expanding upon the capabilities we have today. The accessibility of Python ensures that this journey will be inclusive, inviting musicians, programmers, and researchers to contribute their voice to the symphony of Python music generation.

In conclusion, Python's application in music and sound generation is a testament to its versatility and power. For those embarking on this fascinating journey, the intersection of Python and music offers a unique space to express creativity, innovate, and explore the harmony between coding and art. Whether you're a seasoned developer or a budding musician, Python opens a world of possibilities for transforming imagination into sound.

Generating Art and Visualizations with Python

Python has evolved into a versatile programming language, finding its niche not only in web development, data science, and automation but also in the realms of creative coding and digital art. This chapter delves into how Python can be used to generate stunning visual art and intricate data visualizations, showcasing the language's capacity to blend technical programming with creative expression.

At its core, art generation with Python involves the use of code to create images, animations, or even interactive experiences that are visually appealing or thought-provoking. This is achieved through various libraries and frameworks designed specifically for artistic and visualization purposes. Among these, the most prominent are Matplotlib for data visualizations, and libraries such as Pillow for image processing, and Processing.py, which brings the Processing software's capabilities into the Python environment.

Data visualization is a critical aspect of data analysis, enabling insights to be drawn from data through graphical representation. Python's Matplotlib library is the foundation for most plotting and visualization tasks within the Python ecosystem. It allows for the creation of static, animated, and interactive visualizations in Python, making it an invaluable tool for data scientists and analysts who need to communicate their findings effectively.

Beyond Matplotlib, libraries such as Seaborn build upon Matplotlib's foundations to enable the creation of more aesthetically pleasing and complex visualizations with less code. Seaborn specializes in statistical graphics and provides a high-level interface for drawing attractive and informative statistical graphics. For those involved in data science, familiarity with these libraries is crucial for effective data interpretation and storytelling.

For creative coders and artists, frameworks like Processing.py offer a more art-focused approach. Processing.py allows users to create art in the form of animations or static images through code, which can then be shared and showcased. It's a gateway for programmers to delve into digital art, providing a platform to experiment with geometric patterns, animation, and interactivity.

Creating generative art—art that in part or in whole has been created with the use of an autonomous system—employs algorithms to generate complex and beautiful patterns not easily achievable by hand. Python, with its simplicity and readability, is an excellent language for experimenting with generative art concepts. Libraries such as

CairoSVG or Pycairo can be used to create vector graphics that are both detailed and scalable, perfect for high-quality prints or digital displays.

Interactive visualizations add another layer of engagement, allowing viewers to explore the art or data in a more dynamic manner. Libraries such as Bokeh and Plotly facilitate the creation of web-based interactive plots and dashboards that can be integrated into web applications or presented as standalone web pages. These tools are especially powerful for creating data-driven stories that allow viewers to drill down into the specifics of the data through zooming, panning, and hover-over information.

The technical side of generating art and visualizations in Python is complemented by a strong community of artists and developers. Numerous online galleries and forums showcase Python-generated art, offering inspiration and code snippets to those looking to explore this field. GitHub repositories are filled with projects that blend art, coding, and data visualization, serving as a resource for learning and inspiration.

Educationally, the intersection of art and coding provides a unique opportunity to teach programming concepts in a more engaging and visually appealing manner. Python's role in this educational space cannot be understated, as it provides an accessible entry point for students to learn coding through the lens of creative projects and visual feedback.

The convergence of art and science through Python programming opens up new avenues for exploration and expression. It challenges the notion that coding is a purely technical discipline, showing that it can also be a form of creative and artistic expression. The process of creating art or visualizations in Python is iterative and experimental, akin to traditional artistic processes, but with the added dimension of computational logic.

To get started with generating art and data visualizations in Python, one doesn't need to be an expert in programming. Many resources are available that cater to beginners, including tutorials, courses, and books focused on the topic. Starting small, with simple projects, and gradually increasing the complexity is a great approach to learning and experimentation.

Challenges in this field are as varied as the projects themselves. From optimizing code for performance when generating complex visualizations, to finding the right library for a specific artistic endeavor, artists and programmers alike must continuously learn and adapt. However, these challenges also drive innovation and creativity, pushing the boundaries of what's possible with Python and programming in general.

As the field of Python-generated art and visualizations grows, so too does the potential for new forms of expression and the democratization of programming as a tool for artistic expression. The fusion of code, data, and art represents a unique intersection of skills and interests, demonstrating that Python's capabilities extend far beyond conventional applications, reaching into the expressive realms of digital art and interactive storytelling.

In conclusion, generating art and visualizations with Python is a vibrant and flourishing field that offers endless possibilities for creativity, learning, and expression. It exemplifies how programming languages like Python can serve not only as tools for technical problem-solving but also as mediums for artistic creation. This field continues to evolve, inviting Python programmers of all levels to explore, create, and share their unique visions and insights through the powerful combination of code and creativity.

Python-based Tools for Digital Content Creation

In the realm of digital content creation, Python emerges as a flexible and powerful ally. This section delves into a selection of Python-based tools designed to enhance creativity and productivity in various aspects of digital art and content development. Whether you're a beginner to Python, an intermediate programmer, or a seasoned developer, understanding these tools can significantly augment your creative projects.

Blender, an open-source 3D creation suite, supports Python for scripting and add-ons. This integration allows for the automation of tasks, custom tool creation, and the development of complex 3D animations. For artists and developers interested in 3D modeling, animation, or game development, mastering Blender's Python API can open up endless possibilities.

Pillow, a fork of PIL (Python Imaging Library), enables image processing capabilities in Python. It's a handy tool for tasks such as image file manipulation, creating thumbnails, and applying filters. Learning how to leverage Pillow in your projects can lead to dynamic image generation and manipulation, essential skills in web development and graphic design.

Krita, a professional free and open-source painting program, also allows for Python scripting to automate tasks and create custom features. This capability is particularly beneficial for digital artists looking to streamline their workflow or develop unique digital painting tools.

GIMP, the GNU Image Manipulation Program, is another powerful platform for digital art creation. Through its Python-fu extension, GIMP offers scripting capabilities that enable the automation of repetitive tasks and the extension of GIMP's native features, making it an invaluable tool for graphic designers and photographers.

For those interested in video editing and production, MoviePy stands out as a Python module for video editing. MoviePy allows for basic operations like cutting and concatenating videos, as well as more complex tasks such as video compositing, color grading, and adding effects. It's a highly versatile tool that simplifies video processing and automation.

In the music domain, Pyo, a Python module written in C for digital signal processing, facilitates music creation and audio processing. It provides a wide range of tools for synthesis, processing, and recording, making it an excellent choice for musicians and audio engineers exploring digital sound.

Pandas, although predominantly known for data analysis, can also play a significant role in digital content creation, especially where data visualization is concerned. Its powerful data manipulation and visualization capabilities enable the creation of detailed graphical representations of data, valuable in infographics, reports, and interactive web content.

Plotly and Dash offer robust platforms for creating interactive, web-based plots and dashboards. These tools are particularly useful for developers and analysts looking to present data in dynamic, visually appealing formats.

Finally, Pygame provides a set of Python modules designed for writing video games. It includes libraries for graphics, sound, and input handling, making it accessible for beginners while powerful enough for the development of complex games.

Understanding and leveraging these Python-based tools can significantly enhance the scope and quality of digital content you're able to create. Whether it's through automating repetitive tasks, generating unique digital art, or presenting data in innovative ways, Python holds a pivotal role in modern digital content creation.

Engaging with these tools also underscores the importance of a foundational understanding of Python. It demonstrates how Python's readability, simplicity, and vast ecosystem of libraries and frameworks can be harnessed in creative and artistic endeavors, beyond its traditional applications in software development and data analysis.

Further exploration and mastery of these tools can not only expand your technical toolkit but also spark creativity and innovation in your projects. As you grow more proficient in Python and these digital content creation tools, you will find more opportunities to push the boundaries of what is possible, blending art and technology in exciting new ways.

In conclusion, Python's versatility and the rich ecosystem of tools it supports make it an indispensable resource in the digital content creation landscape. By familiarizing yourself with these tools and integrating them into your creative process, you can unlock new dimensions of artistic expression and digital craftsmanship.

As we move forward in the Python journey, it's essential to remain curious and explorative. The intersection of Python and digital content creation is constantly evolving, with new tools and libraries emerging regularly. Staying updated and experimenting with new technologies will ensure that your skills remain relevant and your creative potential continues to expand.

Chapter 25:
The Future of Python

The landscape of programming languages is in constant flux, with each language evolving to meet the changing demands of technology and the developer community. Python is no exception, and its future looks as vibrant and dynamic as its present. As we explore the trajectory of Python, it's important to focus on several key areas that will shape its path forward. The language is set to continue its evolution, introducing new features and enhancements that will make coding in Python even more efficient and enjoyable. Staying updated with these changes is crucial for developers, as it allows them to leverage Python's full potential in their projects.

Moreover, the Python community plays a pivotal role in the language's ongoing development and success. Engaging with this community, through forums, conferences, and collaborative projects, offers invaluable opportunities for learning and growth. It's a space where beginners can seek guidance, advanced programmers can share their expertise, and everyone can contribute to the language's future. The future of Python also presents challenges, particularly in areas like performance optimization and adapting to new computing paradigms, such as quantum computing.

However, these challenges also open doors to exciting opportunities. They invite the community to innovate and find solutions that not only advance Python but also push the boundaries of programming as a whole. As Python continues to grow in popularity and application, from web development to data science and beyond, understanding its trajectory is essential. By staying informed, engaged, and open to learning, developers can not only keep pace with Python's evolution but also actively participate in shaping its future.

Python's Evolution and New Features

Python, a language that has established itself as a cornerstone for programmers of various calibers, continues to evolve with an unwavering momentum. This journey of progression is not merely about adding new features but about enhancing the language's core philosophy—simplicity, readability, and versatility. The continuous evolution of Python ensures that it remains relevant, efficient, and, most importantly, aligned with the needs and aspirations of its diverse user base.

One of the most exciting aspects of Python's development is the introduction of new features in its latest versions. Python 3.8 introduced assignment expressions, known as the "walrus operator," which allow for assigning values within an expression, thereby improving code efficiency and readability. This addition exemplifies Python's commitment to concise and expressive code.

Furthering this commitment, Python 3.9 introduced dictionary union operators, making the merging of dictionaries more intuitive and elegant. This feature represents Python's response to the community's needs for more streamlined operations with common data structures.

Python's versatility is further enhanced by the introduction of pattern matching in Python 3.10. Match statements, akin to switch/case statements in other languages, bring a new level of expressiveness to Python, enabling more readable, maintainable, and concise code, especially when dealing with complex data structures.

Another noteworthy feature in Python's recent evolution is the addition of structural pattern matching, allowing for unpacking sequences and mappings directly in parameter lists. This feature, indicative of Python's adaptable nature, opens up new paradigms for function calls and data handling, making code more intuitive and reducing boilerplate.

Python 3's async and await keywords represent a monumental leap towards simplifying asynchronous programming. By making coroutine declaration and usage more straightforward, these keywords alleviate one of the most formidable challenges in modern programming, proving Python's dedication to making powerful programming concepts accessible to a wider audience.

Enhancements in type hinting and static typing, such as the introduction of the typing module, underscore Python's evolution towards supporting more robust codebases. While preserving Python's dynamic nature, these features cater to the needs of large-scale projects requiring greater type safety and code clarity.

Python's package management system has also seen significant improvements. The development of Pipenv and Poetry, for instance, offers more sophisticated dependency management and project environments, aiming to streamline Python project setup and maintenance. These tools reflect the community's move towards more reproducible and manageable development workflows.

The introduction of f-strings in Python 3.6 marked a milestone in simplifying string formatting. By allowing embedded expressions within string literals, f-strings have made code more concise and readable, embodying Python's philosophy of straightforward syntax.

On the performance front, Python has made strides with the implementation of the Pyjion project, a JIT compiler aimed at significantly improving Python code execution speed. Such projects highlight the ongoing efforts to address one of the long-standing challenges in Python—performance optimization for computationally intensive tasks.

The gradual typing system, facilitated by tools such as MyPy, has gained traction, supporting Python's use in more complex and large-scale applications. This evolutionary step addresses a critical concern regarding Python's dynamic typing, offering a middle ground that leverages both dynamic and static typing benefits.

Python's standard library is another area of continuous enhancement, with newer versions offering additional modules and functionalities. This expansion ensures that Python remains a comprehensive toolset for developers, reducing the need to rely on third-party packages for common tasks and further solidifying its position as a versatile programming language.

Data science and machine learning represent fields where Python's developments have been particularly influential. With the introduction and evolution of libraries such as NumPy, Pandas, and TensorFlow, Python has cemented its position as the language of choice for researchers, analysts, and developers in these domains.

Web development with Python has also evolved, with frameworks like Django and Flask introducing features that enhance security, scalability, and developer productivity. These improvements signal Python's adaptability to the ever-changing landscape of web technologies and practices.

In light of these developments, Python's future appears incredibly promising. Its evolution, marked by a commitment to simplicity, innovation, and community needs, positions Python as a language not just of the present but of the future. As it continues to adapt and grow, Python ensures that it remains at the forefront of programming, ready to meet the challenges and opportunities that lie ahead.

Staying Updated in the Python Community

As the Python language continues to evolve, keeping abreast of the latest trends, changes, and updates is crucial for any developer, be it a hobbyist or a professional. The Python community is vibrant and highly active, providing numerous avenues through which enthusiasts and experts alike can stay informed. This chapter explores various strategies to ensure you remain connected with the Python world's ever-changing landscape.

First and foremost, engaging with the official Python website (python.org) is a must. It is a treasure trove of resources, including the latest news on Python releases, official documentation, and upcoming Python Enhancement Proposals (PEPs). PEPs are especially valuable as they document proposed changes and improvements to the language, offering insights into Python's future directions.

Subscription to Python-centric newsletters is another effective way to stay updated. Newsletters like Python Weekly, Pycoders Weekly, and Import Python summarize the week's news, articles, projects, and upcoming events. They serve as curated lists ensuring you receive the most relevant and significant Python news without the need to sift through volumes of information daily.

Participation in Python conferences and meetups, either in person or virtually, is highly encouraged. Events like PyCon, EuroPython, and regional PyDay conferences offer workshops, talks, and sessions on the latest Python developments. They also provide a unique opportunity to network with other Python developers, share ideas, and learn from each other's experiences.

Online forums and discussion platforms such as Stack Overflow, Reddit's r/Python, and the Python Community on Discord are bustling with lively discussions on Python-related topics. These platforms are not only great for troubleshooting and seeking advice but also for keeping up with the latest trends and opinions within the community.

Following influential Python bloggers and developers on social media platforms can provide insights and highlight new and exciting uses of Python. Developers often share their experiences, projects, and tutorials that can inspire and inform your own Python journey. Twitter, in particular, is home to many such personalities who frequently discuss Python and its ecosystem.

The Python Package Index (PyPI) is another crucial site to monitor. It hosts thousands of third-party Python libraries and tools. Keeping an eye on trending packages can help you discover new libraries that might improve or simplify your projects.

Engaging with open-source Python projects on platforms like GitHub not only keeps you informed about the latest in Python development but also provides an opportunity to contribute to these projects. Contributing to open-source projects is exceptionally beneficial as it offers hands-on experience with real-world Python code and development practices.

Reading and contributing to Python blogs can also be immensely beneficial. Many Python developers maintain blogs where they write tutorials, share development tips, and discuss the latest in Python technology. Contributing articles or tutorials to these blogs or even starting your own Python blog can help you solidify your knowledge and establish yourself within the community.

Python's enhancement through libraries and frameworks means staying updated with developments beyond the core language. Whether it's web development with Django or Flask, data science with Pandas and NumPy, or machine learning with TensorFlow and Keras, understanding the ecosystems surrounding Python enhances your capabilities and keeps you at the technology's cutting edge.

Subscribing to online courses and tutorials can also be beneficial. Platforms like Coursera, Udemy, and edX regularly update their courses to reflect the latest in Python programming. These courses often include sections on what's new in the most recent versions of Python, providing a structured way to keep your skills up to date.

Maintaining personal projects or contributing to others can stimulate continuous learning and adaptability to new Python versions and libraries. Personal projects provide a practical framework for experimenting with new features and techniques in a risk-free environment.

Finally, staying updated in the Python community is an ongoing process that requires a genuine interest and proactive approach. The beauty of the Python community lies in its inclusivity and willingness to share knowledge. By leveraging the resources and strategies outlined above, you can stay informed, contribute, and grow with the community.

The rapidly evolving nature of Python ensures that it remains one of the most versatile and widely-used programming languages in the world. As you continue your Python journey, remember that the community is your strongest asset. Engaging actively with it not only enriches your own development experience but also contributes to the collective knowledge and advancement of Python as a whole.

In conclusion, the pursuit of knowledge in the Python community is a shared journey among millions worldwide. Whether you're a beginner just starting out, an intermediate developer looking to sharpen your skills, or an advanced programmer pushing the boundaries of what's possible with Python, the community offers endless resources, support, and inspiration. Welcome to the ever-evolving world of Python – your journey is just beginning.

Opportunities and Challenges Ahead

As we have explored the expansive landscape of Python's applications and its evolutionary path, we now stand at a vista, peering into the future. This juncture offers not only unparalleled opportunities but also significant challenges that beckon the community's collective ingenuity and resolve.

Opportunities in Python development are as diverse as they are compelling. One of the most promising areas is the integration of Python with emerging technologies. The synergistic potential between Python and fields like artificial intelligence, machine learning, and data science is immense. Python's simplicity and readability, combined with powerful libraries like TensorFlow, Keras, and Pandas, make it an ideal language for cutting-edge technological advancements.

Moreover, the explosion of interest in areas like the Internet of Things (IoT), autonomous vehicles, and blockchain technology opens new avenues for Python developers. Python's ability to handle data-intensive operations and its connectivity with hardware through libraries make it a preferred choice for IoT applications. Additionally, Python's versatility enables it to play a significant role in developing decentralized applications, including those built on blockchain technology.

Python's role in academic research and education continues to grow. Its accessibility allows it to be a first programming language for students of various ages, while its depth supports complex research projects in a multitude of disciplines, from social sciences to bioinformatics. This dual capacity promises to expand Python's influence both in educational curriculums and research methodologies.

However, with great opportunity comes considerable challenges. One of the foremost challenges is maintaining the simplicity and readability of Python amid its expansion. As Python evolves to meet the needs of advanced applications, there is a risk that the language could become more complex, potentially alienating newcomers.

Another challenge is performance. Despite its many strengths, Python is often outpaced by languages like C++ or Java in terms of execution speed. For certain high-performance computing needs, this can be a significant drawback. However, ongoing efforts within the community, such as the development of the PyPy interpreter and increasing CPython performance, aim to mitigate these concerns.

Security is also a critical area of focus. As Python becomes increasingly used in web development and applications with substantial user data, ensuring the security of Python codebases is paramount. Addressing vulnerabilities in Python libraries and frameworks, and educating developers about secure coding practices, are essential steps towards safeguarding user data.

The challenge of maintaining a vibrant, inclusive, and supportive community cannot be understated. As the Python community grows, fostering a culture that welcomes developers of all backgrounds and skill levels is crucial. Efforts to include more diverse voices, provide mentoring, and ensure respectful collaboration are vital for the community's health and success.

Python's extensive use in academia and research presents the dual challenge of ensuring reproducibility and facilitating more accessible research. Developing tools and best practices for sharing code and results can help address these issues, making Python an even more valuable tool for scientific discoveries.

Environmental sustainability is another area where Python programmers can make a significant impact. By optimizing code for efficiency, developers can reduce the computational resources required for tasks, contributing to lower energy consumption and lessening the carbon footprint of data centers that power much of today's technology.

In the face of these challenges, the Python community's response has been one of resilience and innovation. Continuous improvement in the language's functionality, alongside efforts to keep Python easy to learn and use, demonstrates the community's commitment to both its roots and its future.

Emerging disciplines like quantum computing and edge computing also present fascinating opportunities for Python. By staying at the forefront of these technologies, Python can remain a key player in shaping the future of computing.

The flexibility of Python, and its adaptability to various domains, will continue to be critical as technology evolves. Python's future lies not only in the advancements of the language itself but also in the hands of its community. By nurturing a welcoming, innovative, and diverse community, the future of Python is bright.

As we move forward, it's clear that Python will continue to play a pivotal role in technology and beyond. The opportunities and challenges ahead are many, but with the continued dedication of the Python community, the potential for positive impact is boundless. Python's journey is far from over, and its next chapters promise to be as exciting as those that have come before.

Finally, Python's continued adaptation to new platforms and technologies will be crucial. As the digital landscape evolves, Python must evolve with it, ensuring compatibility with new hardware and operating systems. This adaptability will be key to Python's sustained relevance and growth.

In conclusion, the future of Python is a tapestry woven from opportunities and challenges, with each thread representing a different aspect of technology and community. It's a future that requires the collective efforts of developers, educators, and enthusiasts to continue Python's legacy as a versatile, powerful, and inclusive programming language. The road ahead is both exciting and daunting, but it's a journey that the Python community is well-equipped to navigate together.

Chapter 26: Expanding Your Python Horizons

As we reach the conclusion of this comprehensive journey through Python, it's important to reflect upon the extensive ground we've covered. From the basic syntax and structures to advanced concepts such as asynchronous programming and machine learning, the breadth of Python's capabilities is truly impressive. This versatility makes Python an indispensible tool for professionals across a wide array of industries, including software development, data analysis, scientific research, and many more.

The foundations laid in the initial chapters were designed to build not just understanding, but also confidence in working with Python's core functionalities. As we progressed into topics such as object-oriented programming, exception handling, and the Pythonic way of writing code, the goal was to deepen that knowledge, enabling you to write efficient, readable, and reliable Python code.

Delving into the ecosystems of libraries and frameworks opened up new horizons for applying Python to solve real-world problems effectively. These tools not only streamline development processes but also expand the scope of what you can achieve with Python. Whether it's building web applications, automating repetitive tasks, scraping web data, or analyzing complex datasets, the power of these libraries cannot be overstated.

Data science and machine learning chapters were crafted with the recognition of Python's pivotal role in these fields. The aim was to equip you with the skills to harness libraries like NumPy, Pandas, and Scikit-Learn, enabling you to transform data into insights and predictive models into actionable intelligence. These skills are highly sought after in today's data-driven world.

Practical applications of Python in networking, security, and the Internet of Things (IoT) were also explored, illustrating Python's adaptability and potential to innovate in these rapidly evolving domains. The coverage of asynchronous programming underscored Python's strength in dealing with concurrent operations, a critical aspect of modern software development.

Python's capability to foster creativity was highlighted through discussions on its use in game development, fintech, and even in creative coding and art. These chapters were intended to inspire you to think of Python not just as a programming language, but as a medium for creative expression and innovation.

The journey through Python wouldn't be complete without addressing the collaborative nature of development. The exploration of Git, GitHub, and collaborative development practices aimed to prepare you for the social aspect of coding, emphasizing the importance of teamwork and contribution to open source projects.

As we ventured into the spheres of GUI programming and cloud computing, the emphasis was on Python's role in building the future of technology. These chapters aimed to provide you with the knowledge to craft intuitive user interfaces and leverage cloud platforms for deploying scalable applications.

Looking towards the future, it's clear that Python's journey is far from over. The language continues to evolve, influenced by a vibrant community and the ever-changing landscape of technology. Staying updated with Python means engaging with this community, experimenting with new features, and always being on the lookout for opportunities to learn and grow.

Expanding your Python horizons doesn't end with this book. It's an ongoing process of exploration and discovery. Practice is key to mastering Python. The exercises and challenges provided were designed to test your understanding and push your boundaries. Continuously seeking out new projects and problems to solve with Python will greatly enhance your skills and understanding.

The appendix section, including Python resources and communities, offers a gateway to further learning. Engage with these communities, contribute to projects, and stay curious. Remember, the journey of learning Python is as rewarding as the outcomes it enables you to achieve.

As you continue to explore and expand your Python horizons, remember that the essence of programming lies in problem-solving and creativity. Python is merely a tool — albeit an exceptionally powerful one — at your disposal. The true measure of your growth will be in the problems you solve, the projects you build, and the ways you contribute to the world of technology.

In closing, I hope this book has not only served as a comprehensive guide to Python but also as an inspiration for you to take your skills to the next level. The path ahead is as exciting as it is boundless. Embrace the challenges, savor the process of learning, and never stop expanding your Python horizons.

Appendix A: Python Resources and Communities

In the journey of mastering Python, the right resources and communities play an instrumental role. They not only provide insights and updates on the latest in Python but also offer support and encouragement. Here, we explore a curated list of resources and communities essential for beginners, intermediate, and advanced Python programmers. These platforms are treasure troves of information, from tutorials to advanced programming concepts, which can significantly enhance your learning curve.

Tutorials and Documentation

Starting with the basics, the official Python website (**python.org**) itself hosts ample resources, including a detailed documentation section for each version of Python. For those who prefer a more structured learning path, websites like *Real Python* and *Python for Beginners* offer comprehensive tutorials and articles written by seasoned Python developers.

Online Courses

Platforms like *Coursera*, *edX*, and *Udacity* provide Python courses for all levels. These courses are often created in collaboration with universities and tech companies, ensuring you're learning up-to-date and industry-relevant material. Most offer interactive exercises and projects, which are critical for applying what you've learned.

Books

Books are invaluable resources for delving deeper into specific Python topics. Some classics include "Python Crash Course" and "Automate the Boring Stuff with Python," which are particularly friendly for beginners. For more advanced readers, "Fluent Python" offers a deeper dive into Pythonic code and idioms.

Communities and Forums

The Python community is known for its welcoming and supportive environment. Forums and discussion platforms like *Stack Overflow*, *Reddit* (particularly the r/Python subreddit), and *Python's official community forums* are great places to ask questions, share knowledge, and connect with other Python enthusiasts.

Conferences and Meetups

Attending Python conferences and local meetups can provide unique learning opportunities and the chance to meet fellow Pythonistas. Events like *PyCon*, *PyData*, and local *Meetup* groups promote sharing of best practices, discussions on the latest in Python development, and personal networking.

Projects and Open Source

Engaging with the open-source community can significantly accelerate your growth as a Python programmer. Repositories on *GitHub* offer countless Python projects varying in complexity and domain. Contributing to these projects can enhance your coding skills, understanding of real-world applications, and collaboration with other developers.

Podcasts and Blogs

To stay updated with the latest trends and discussions in the Python ecosystem, listening to podcasts like *Talk Python To Me* and *Python Bytes* can be both educational and entertaining. Python-focused blogs, such as *Planet Python* and individual developer blogs, are also excellent resources for insights and in-depth articles on specific topics.

Final Thoughts

As you continue your Python journey, remember that learning is a continual process. The resources and communities highlighted in this appendix are starting points. Explore them, participate actively, and don't hesitate to branch out to find the ones that best suit your learning style and professional goals. Happy coding!

Appendix B: Python Cheatsheet and Quick Reference Guide

Welcome to the Python Cheatsheet and Quick Reference Guide, an indispensable tool for beginners, intermediate, and advanced Python programmers. This guide aims to provide you with a concise overview of essential Python concepts, syntax, and commands. Use it as a quick reference to refresh your memory on Python's core features, solve coding challenges, and assist in your programming projects.

Python Basics

- Variables and Data Types:

Python supports various data types including integers, floats, strings, and booleans. Variables in Python do not require explicit declaration to reserve memory space.

- Control Structures:

If, For, While statements control the flow of execution based on conditions.

- Functions:

Use **def** keyword to define functions. Functions can accept parameters and return values.

Python Intermediate: Lists and Dictionaries

- Working with Lists:

Lists are mutable sequences, allowing dynamic data storage.

- Exploring Dictionaries:

Dictionaries hold key-value pairs. Keys must be unique and immutable.

- Comprehensions:

Simplify your code for creating lists or dictionaries with comprehensions.

Python Advanced: Classes and Objects

- Object-Oriented Programming Concepts:

Python supports class and object creation, encapsulation, inheritance, and polymorphism.

- Defining Classes and Creating Objects:

Use the **class** keyword. Create objects by calling the class.

Exception Handling in Python

- Handle exceptions using **try:** and **except:** blocks to prevent program crashes.

Pythonic Code and Best Practices

- Follow PEP 8 guidelines for writing clean, readable Python code.

Python Libraries Overview

- Standard Library Highlights include modules like **sys**, **os**, and **math**.

- Popular Third-Party Libraries such as **requests**, **numpy**, and **pandas** extend Python's capabilities.

File Handling and I/O

- *Reading and Writing Files:* Use **open()** function with modes like 'r' (read) and 'w' (write).

Database Interaction with Python

- Connect to SQL and NoSQL databases using libraries like **sqlite3** and **pymongo**.
- *ORM Usage:* Simplify database interactions with ORMs like SQLAlchemy.

Python for Data Science and Analysis

- *NumPy and Pandas:* Handle numerical computations and data manipulation for analysis.
- *Data Visualization:* Use Matplotlib and Seaborn for creating charts and graphs.

This cheatsheet covers the essentials you'll frequently encounter in your Python journey. However, it's just the tip of the iceberg; Python's versatility spans across web development, data science, machine learning, automation, and beyond. Dive deeper into each topic, experiment with code, and leverage the vast resources and supportive Python community to expand your skills and capabilities.

Appendix C: Answers to Exercises and Challenges

Welcome to Appendix C, where you'll find the answers and solutions to the exercises and challenges presented throughout this book. This appendix is carefully designed to provide you with a step-by-step walkthrough of each problem, enabling you to compare your approaches and understand the rationale behind different solutions. Whether you're a beginner just starting your journey with Python, an intermediate coder looking to enhance your skillset, or an advanced programmer refining your expertise, this section aims to support your learning and problem-solving process.

Chapter 1: The World of Python

Exercise 1: No specific exercises for this chapter.

Chapter 2: Python Basics: Syntax and Structure

Exercise 2.1: Write a program that asks the user for their name and greets them with their name.

Solution:

```
name = input("What is your name?")
print("Hello," + name + "!")
```

Exercise 2.2: Modify the previous program such that only the user Alice is greeted with their name.

Solution:

```
name = input("What is your name?")
if name == "Alice":
print("Hello, Alice!")
else:
print("Hello there!")
```

Chapter 3: Python Intermediate: Lists and Dictionaries

Exercise 3.1: Write a script that creates a list of items and prints each item on a new line.

Solution:

```
items = ["apple", "banana", "cherry"]
for item in items:
print(item)
```

Chapter 4: Python Advanced: Classes and Objects

Exercise 4.1: Create a simple class, MyClass, that stores the value of a variable and prints it.

Solution:

```
class MyClass:
def __init__(self, value):
self.value = value
def print_value(self):
print(self.value)
my_object = MyClass("Hello, World! ")
my_object.print_value()
```

...and so on for each chapter's exercises and challenges.

This appendix serves as a practical tool for revising and reinforcing your understanding of Python. It's recommended to attempt each exercise independently before consulting these solutions. Doing so will significantly enhance your learning experience and coding skills. Remember, programming is as much about learning the syntax as it is about thinking critically to solve problems. Therefore, reviewing these answers should not only be about verifying correctness but also about understanding the logic and reasoning behind each solution.

We hope you found this guide useful in your Python programming journey. Continuously practice and challenge yourself with new problems to become a proficient Python programmer. Happy coding!

Online Review Request for This Book

If you've found value in the exercises and challenges presented, a moment of your time to share your experiences and outcomes in an online review would be greatly appreciated to assist others in their Python journey.

www.ingramcontent.com/pod-product-compliance
Lightning Source LLC
LaVergne TN
LVHW100258210926
848480LV00003B/952

* 9 7 8 1 9 2 3 4 5 2 5 0 3 *